SUMMER EXPRESS

GRADES K&1

NEW YORK • TORONTO • LONDON • AUCKLAND • SYDNEY
MEXICO CITY • NEW DELHI • HONG KONG • BUENOS AIRES

Cover design by Brian LaRossa
Cover photo by Ariel Skelley/Corbis
Interior illustrations by Robert Alley, Abbey Carter, Maxie Chambliss, Sue Dennen,
Shelley Dieterichs, Jane Dippold, Julie Durrell, Rusty Fletcher, James Hale,
Mike Moran, Sherry Neidigh, Cary Pillo, Carol Tiernon, and Lynn Vineyard

ISBN-13 978-0-545-22690-5 / ISBN-10 0-545-22690-2

Table of Contents

Dear Parent:

Congratulations! You hold in your hands an exceptional educational tool that will give your child a head start into the coming school year.

Inside this book, you'll find one hundred practice pages that will help your child review and learn reading and writing skills, grammar, addition and subtraction, and so much more! *Summer Express* is divided into 10 weeks, with two practice pages for each day of the week, Monday to Friday. However, feel free to use the pages in any order that your child would like. Here are other features you'll find inside:

• A weekly **incentive chart** and **certificate** to motivate and reward your child for his or her efforts.

• A sheet of **colorful stickers**. There are small stickers for completing the activities each day, as well as a large sticker to use as a weekly reward.

• Suggestions for fun, creative **learning activities** you can do with your child each week.

• A **recommended reading list** of age-appropriate books that you and your child can read throughout the summer.

• A **certificate of completion** to celebrate your child's accomplishments.

We hope you and your child will have a lot of fun as you work together to complete this workbook.

Enjoy!
The editors

Terrific Tips for Using This Book

1 Pick a good time for your child to work on the activities. You may want to do it around mid-morning after play, or early afternoon when your child is not too tired.

2 Make sure your child has all the supplies he or she needs, such as pencils and crayons. Set aside a special place for your child to work.

3 At the beginning of each week, discuss with your child how many minutes a day he or she would like to read. Write the goal at the top of the incentive chart for the week. (We recommend reading 10 to 15 minutes a day with your child who is entering 1st grade.)

4 To celebrate your child's accomplishments, let him or her affix stickers on the incentive chart for completing the activities each day. Reward your child's reading efforts with a bonus sticker at the end of the week as well.

5 Encourage your child to complete the worksheet, but don't force the issue. While you may want to ensure that your child succeeds, it's also important that he or she maintain a positive and relaxed attitude toward school and learning.

6 After you've given your child a few minutes to look over the practice pages he or she will be working on, ask your child to tell you his or her plan of action: "Tell me about what we're doing on these pages." Hearing the explanation aloud can provide you with insights into your child's thinking processes. Can he or she complete the work independently? With guidance? If your child needs support, try offering a choice regarding which family member might help. Giving your child a choice can help boost confidence and help him or her feel more ownership of the work to be done.

7 When your child has finished the workbook, present him or her with the certificate of completion on page 143. Feel free to frame or laminate the certificate and display it on the wall for everyone to see. Your child will be so proud!

Skill-Building Activities for Any Time

The following activities are designed to complement the ten weeks of practice pages in this book. These activities don't take more than a few minutes to complete and are just a handful of ways in which you can enrich and enliven your child's learning. Use the activities to take advantage of the time you might ordinarily disregard—for example, standing in line or waiting at a bus stop. You'll be working to practice key skills and have fun together at the same time.

Finding Real-Life Connections

One of the reasons for schooling is to help children function out in the real world, to empower them with the abilities they'll truly need. So why not put those developing skills into action by enlisting your child's help with creating a grocery list, reading street signs, sorting pocket change, and so on? He or she can apply reading, writing, science, and math skills in important and practical ways, connecting what he or she is learning with everyday tasks.

An Eye for Patterns

A red-brick sidewalk, a beaded necklace, a Sunday newspaper—all show evidence of structure and organization. You can help your child recognize something's structure or organization by observing and talking about patterns they see. Your child will apply his or her developing ability to spot patterns across all school subject areas, including alphabet letter formation (writing), attributes of shapes and solids (geometry), and characteristics of narrative stories (reading). Being able to notice patterns is a skill shared by effective readers and writers, scientists, and mathematicians.

Journals as Learning Tools

Most of us associate journal writing with reading comprehension, but having your child keep a journal can help you keep up with his or her developing skills in other academic areas as well—from telling time to matching rhymes. To get started, provide your child with several sheets of paper, folded in half, and stapled together. Explain that he or she will be writing and/or drawing in the journal to complement the practice pages completed each week. Encourage your child to draw or write about what he or she found easy, what was difficult, or what was fun. Before moving on to another set of practice pages, take a few minutes to read and discuss that week's journal entries together.

Promote Reading at Home

◆ Let your child catch you in the act of reading for pleasure, whether you like reading science fiction novels or do-it-yourself magazines. Store them someplace that encourages you to read in front of your child and **demonstrate that reading is an activity you enjoy**. For example, locate your reading materials on the coffee table instead of your nightstand.

◆ Set aside a family reading time. By designating a reading time each week, your family is assured an opportunity to discuss with each other what you're reading. You can, for example, share a funny quote from an article. Or your child can tell you his or her favorite part of a story. The key is to **make a family tradition of reading and sharing books** of all kinds together.

◆ **Put together collections of reading materials** your child can access easily. Gather them in baskets or bins that you can place in the family room, the car, and your child's bedroom. You can refresh your child's library by borrowing materials from your community's library, buying used books, or swapping books and magazines with friends and neighbors.

Skills Review and Practice

Educators have established learning standards for math and language arts. Listed below are some of the important skills covered in *Summer Express* that will help your child review and prepare for the coming school year so that he or she is better prepared to meet these learning standards.

Math

Skills Your Child Will Review

- matching numerals to quantities
- recognizing shapes
- identifying patterns

Skills Your Child Will Practice to Prepare for Grade One

- identifying numerals 11–20
- counting quantities to 20
- recognizing fractions
- using addition
- using subtraction
- measuring (e.g., length, time, money)
- estimating quantity
- using number sense
- collecting data
- continuing patterns

Language Arts

Skills Your Child Will Review

- understanding that illustration complements storytelling
- writing upper- and lowercase alphabet letters in manuscript writing
- writing the numerals 1–10 in manuscript writing
- using phonetic analysis (e.g., initial consonants) to match initial consonants with pictured items
- identifying some familiar words in print (e.g., colors, shapes)
- using meaning clues (e.g., illustrations) and phonetic analysis to decode unfamiliar words
- identifying rhyming words and rhyming sounds
- uses visual discrimination to identify similarities and differences in illustrations that do not accompany text

Skills Your Child Will Practice to Prepare for Grade One

- writing familiar vocabulary in manuscript writing (e.g., number words, color words, shape words, days of the week, months of the year)
- using conventions of print in writing (e.g., capitalization and punctuation) to identify and write complete sentences.
- using phonetic analysis (e.g., letter/sound relationships, beginning and ending consonants, short- and long-vowel sounds, consonant blends, digraphs, and word patterns) to decode unfamiliar words
- using structural analysis (e.g., word families) to decode unfamiliar words
- matching phonetically irregular vocabulary (sight words) with level-appropriate list of alike words

Helping Your Child Get Ready: Week 1

These are the skills your child will be working on this week.

Handwriting
- upper- and lowercase letters
- numerals
- number words
- color words

Math
- matching numerals to quantities

Here are some activities you and your child might enjoy.

Laundry Sort When putting away the laundry, enlist your child's help in sorting and matching the socks.

Odd (and Even) Houses As you go for a stroll, point out street addresses in your neighborhood. Guide your child to notice house numbers on one side of the street and compare them with house numbers on the other side. Ask your child what he or she notices about these numbers.

Labels, Labels Everywhere Label different items in your child's room using sticky notes. Encourage your child to read the labels and to help you write some of the labels as well.

Let's Go to the Library Visit your local library and encourage your child to pick a few picture books to borrow.

Your child might enjoy reading the following books:

Art Dog
by Thacher Hurd

Moses Goes to a Concert
by Isaac Millman

's Incentive Chart: Week 1

_____
Name Here

This week, I plan to read_____ minutes each day.

CHART YOUR PROGRESS HERE.

Week 1  I read for...	Day 1	Day 2	Day 3	Day 4	Day 5
	minutes	minutes	minutes	minutes	minutes
Put a sticker to show you completed each day's work.	◯ ◯	◯ ◯	◯ ◯	◯ ◯	◯ ◯

Congratulations!

Wow! You did a great job this week!

Place sticker here.

Parent or Caregiver's Signature_____

A–Z

Trace and write.

A B C D E F G H I

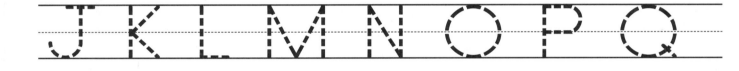

J K L M N O P Q

R S T U V W X Y Z

a–z

Trace and write.

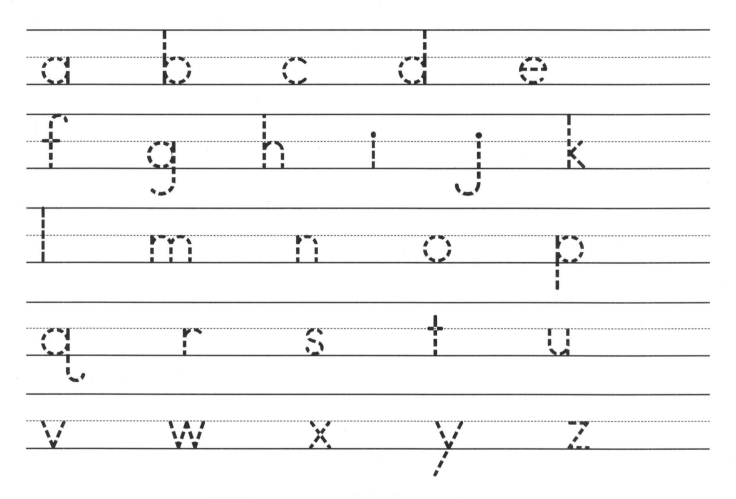

a   b   c   d   e

f   g   h   i   j   k

l   m   n   o   p

q   r   s   t   u

v   w   x   y   z

abcd

1-5

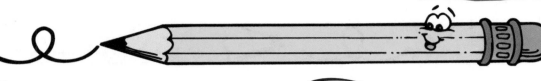

Trace and write.

1

2   2

3   3

4   4

5   5

6-10

Trace and write.

6   6

7   7

8   8

9   9

10   10

Scholastic Inc.   Summer Express: Between Grades K & 1

Number Words

Trace and write.

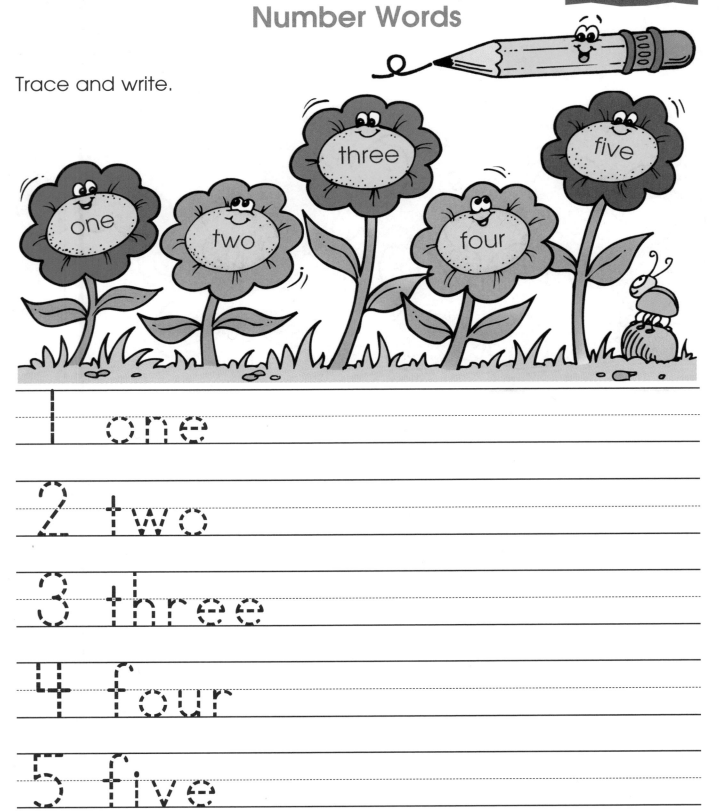

one

two

three

four

five

1 one

2 two

3 three

4 four

5 five

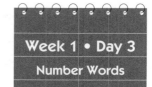

More Number Words

Trace and write.

6 six

7 seven

8 eight

9 nine

10 ten

Scholastic Inc.   Summer Express: Between Grades K & 1

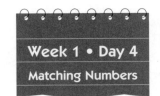

Flowers in a Pot

Count the dots in the boxes. Then color the matching number word using the correct color.

• = green   •• = yellow

••• = red   :: = purple

⁙ = blue

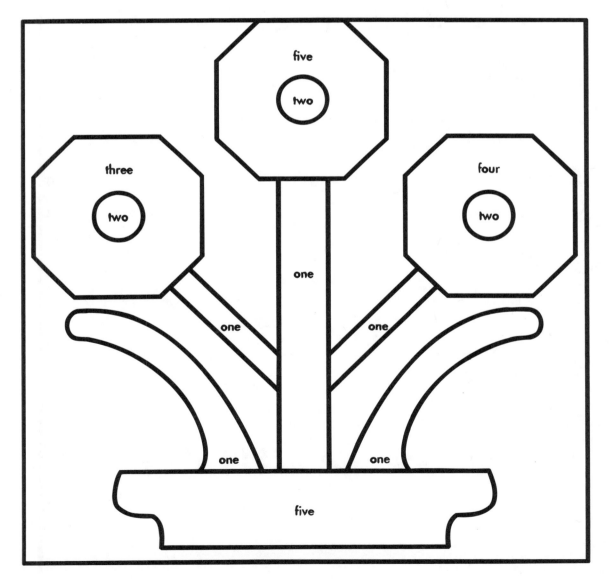

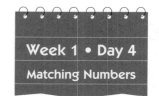

Color the Basket

Count the number of dots or triangles in each shape. Then use the Color Key to tell you what color to make each shape. (For example, a shape with 7 dots will be colored green.)

Color Key
6 = yellow
7 = green
8 = brown
9 = red
10 = blue

Scholastic Inc.   Summer Express: Between Grades K & I

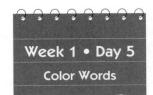

Color Words

Trace and write.

red

yellow

blue

green

orange

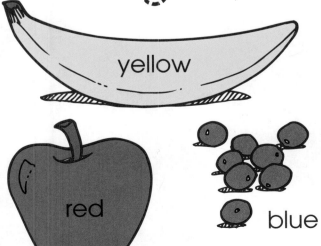

yellow

red

blue

green

orange

More Color Words

Trace and write.

purple

brown

black

white

pink

pink

purple

white

brown

black

Scholastic Inc.   Summer Express: Between Grades K & I

Helping Your Child Get Ready: Week 2

These are the skills your child will be working on this week.

Math
- identifying 11 and 12
- number sense
- recognizing shapes

Reading and Phonics
- initial consonants
- visual discrimination

Handwriting
- shape words
- days of the week

Here are some activities you and your child might enjoy.

Go Right, I Mean, Left! Hide a toy in a room for your child to find. Bring your child into the room and call out direction words, such as left or right, to help your child move toward the toy. Then switch places with your child.

How Many in Our Family? Make counting more meaningful to your child by asking: How many feet are there in our family? How many eyes? How many fingers in our family?

Letter Collection With your child, collect items that start with a particular letter. For example, you might take a book, a ball, and a bell, and put them all in a box labeled B.

How Long Is a Minute? Help your child get a better sense of how long a minute is. Challenge your child to do an activity, such as jumping rope or balancing on one foot, while timing him or her for one minute.

Your child might enjoy reading the following books:

Papa Lucky's Shadow
by Niki Daly

The Art Lesson
by Tomie DePaola

Frog and Toad All Year
by Arnold Lobel

_____ 's Incentive Chart: Week 2

Name Here

This week, I plan to read_____ minutes each day.

CHART YOUR PROGRESS HERE.

Week 2  I read for...	Day 1	Day 2	Day 3	Day 4	Day 5
	minutes	minutes	minutes	minutes	minutes
Put a sticker to show you completed each day's work.					

Congratulations!

Wow! You did a great job this week!

Place sticker here.

Parent or Caregiver's Signature_____

Eleven Excited Earthworms

Trace and write.

| |

Color each set of 11 earthworms.

Twelve Tasty Treats

Trace and write.

12 _____

Count the candy in each jar. Color each jar with 12.

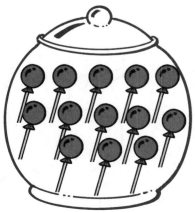

Scholastic Inc.   Summer Express: Between Grades K & 1

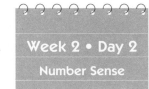

Number User

I use numbers to tell about myself.

1. _____
My
Street Number

2. _____
My
Zip Code

3. _____
My
Telephone Number

4. _____
My
Birthday

5. _____
My
Age

6. _____
My
Height and Weight

7. _____

Number of People in My Family

I can count up to

8. _____

Sign Shape

Street signs come in different shapes. Answer the questions below about the shapes.

1. What shape is this sign? _____

   How many sides does it have? _____

2. What shape is this sign? _____

   How many sides does it have? _____

3. What shape is this sign? _____

   How many sides does it have? _____

4. What shape is this sign? _____

   How many sides does it have? _____

Scholastic Inc.   Summer Express: Between Grades K & I

Food Puzzles

Say the name of each food. Find the letter that stands for the beginning sound of each food. Draw a line from each food to its beginning letter sound.

1.
2.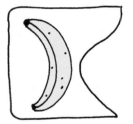
3.
4.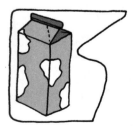
5.

 s

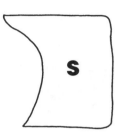 m

 t

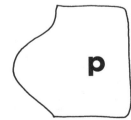 p

 b

Whose Toy Is It?

Read the names on the children's T-shirts aloud. Each child plays only with toys whose names begin with the same sound as his or her name. Fill in the letter that each toy begins with. Then draw lines from each child to the matching toys.

_____ adio   _____ ebra   _____ oll

Dan   Rosa   Zeb

_____ uck   _____ oo   _____ obot

What's Missing?

Look at each set of pictures below. What is missing from the pictures on the right side? Draw what's missing to make both pictures the same.

What's Different?

Look at the top and bottom pictures. Are they exactly the same? Color the three things you see in the bottom picture that are not in the top picture.

Scholastic Inc.   Summer Express: Between Grades K & 1

Shapes

Trace and write.

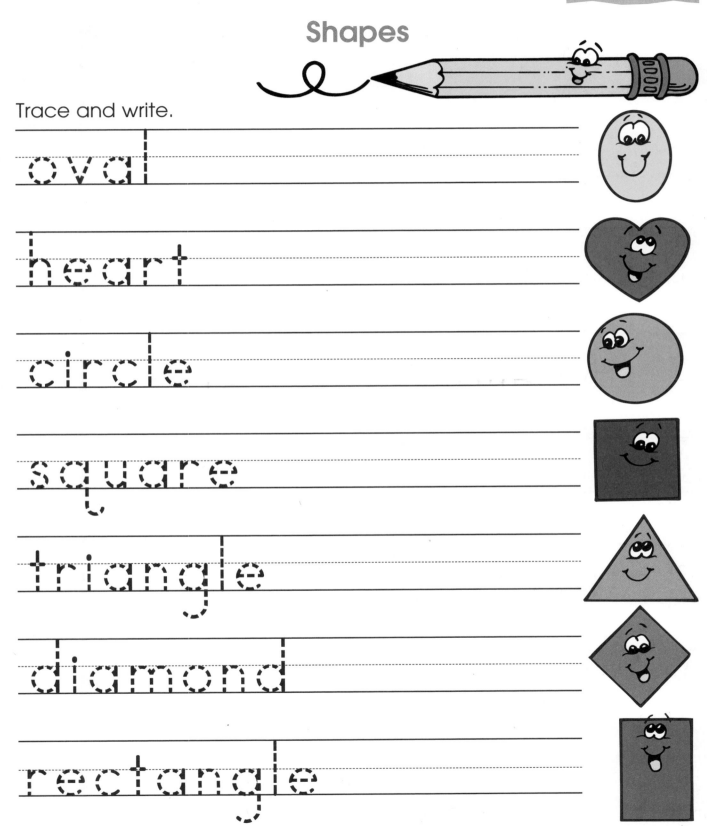

oval

heart

circle

square

triangle

diamond

rectangle

Days of the Week

Trace and write.

Sunday

Monday

Tuesday

Wednesday

Thursday

Friday

Saturday

Scholastic Inc.   Summer Express: Between Grades K & 1

Helping Your Child Get Ready: Week 3

These are the skills your child will be working on this week.

Math
- identifying 13 and 14
- identifying shapes

Reading and Phonics
- initial consonants

Grammar
- capitalization
- identifying sentences

Handwriting
- months

Here are some activities you and your child might enjoy.

Funny Business Read a simple comic strip with your child. Then, cut apart the strip into individual frames and have your child put them back in order.

Books on Tape Tape record yourself reading one of your child's favorite books. Keep the book and tape together so that your child can play the tape and follow the words on the book.

Flip It! Take a deck of playing cards and remove all the jacks, queens, and kings. Distribute the cards evenly between you and your child, making sure to keep the cards facedown. When you say, "Flip it!" both you and your child flip the top card from your pile at the same time. Whoever gets the higher number shouts, "Mine!" and keeps both cards. The person who collects the most cards at the end of the game wins.

Alphabet Counts During snack time, give your child a small cup of alphabet-shaped cereal. Then invite your child to sort the letters and count how many of each letter there are in the cup. You may want to teach your child how to use tally marks to keep a record of each letter.

Your child might enjoy reading the following books:

Crocodile and Hen: A Bakongo Folktale
by Joan M. Lexau

Arrow to the Sun: A Pueblo Indian Tale
by Gerald McDermott

_____
's Incentive Chart: Week 3

This week, I plan to read_____ minutes each day.

CHART YOUR PROGRESS HERE.

Week 3	Day 1	Day 2	Day 3	Day 4	Day 5
 **I read for...**	minutes	minutes	minutes	minutes	minutes
Put a sticker to show you completed each day's work.					

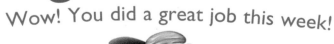

Congratulations!

Wow! You did a great job this week!

Place sticker here.

Parent or Caregiver's Signature_____

Thirteen Tasty Bones

Trace and write.

13

Circle 13 bones in each picture.

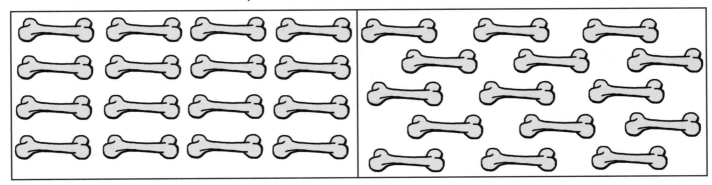

Draw more bones to make 13.

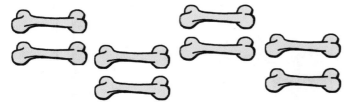

Count the bones. Circle the correct number.　12　13　14

Scholastic Inc.　Summer Express: Between Grades K & 1

Juggling Fourteen Balls

Trace and write.

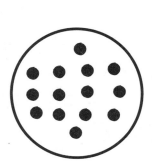

Color each ball with 14 dots.

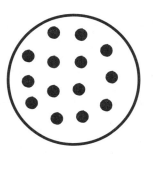

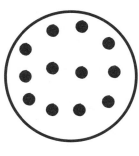

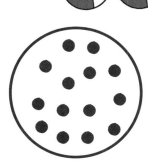

Scholastic Inc.   Summer Express: Between Grades K & 1

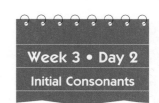
Face First

The pictures show animal faces. Can you name each animal?
Write the letter that each animal's name begins with.

1.  _____

2.  _____

3.  _____

4.  _____

5.  _____

6.  _____

7.  _____

8. _____

What's That Sound?

Say the name of each picture aloud. Choose the letter from the box that stands for the beginning sound of the name. Write it on the line in the speech bubble.

Bb	Pp	Rr	Ww	Yy	Zz

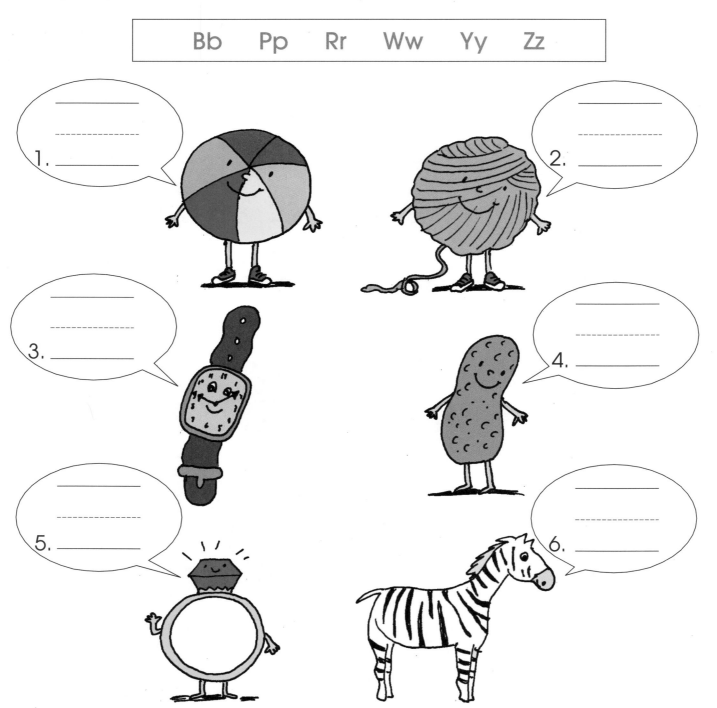

1. _____

2. _____

3. _____

4. _____

5. _____

6. _____

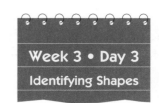
Naming Shapes

1. Draw a line matching each shape to its name.

   triangle

   circle

   square

   rectangle

2. Make an X on the shape that does not belong in the row.

3. Which shape looks like a plate?

4. Which shape has four corners?

5. Which shape looks like an egg?

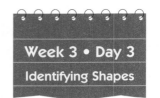
Shapes, Sides, and Corners

Complete the sentences about shapes.

1.

This is a _____.

This shape has _____ sides.

This shape has _____ corners.

2.

This is a _____.

This shape has _____ sides.

This shape has _____ corners.

3.

This is a _____.

This shape has _____ sides.

This shape has _____ corners.

4.

This is a _____.

This shape has _____ sides.

This shape has _____ corners.

---

5. Draw a square. Then draw a line through it to divide it in half to make two rectangles.

6. Draw a square. Then draw a line through it to divide it in half to make two triangles.

That's Amazing!

Help the mouse through the maze by coloring each box with a word that begins with a capital letter.

The	For	That	with	know	but
here	on	When	Have	next	we
as	after	good	Make	there	see
Go	Look	Are	Could	is	why
This	who	said	in	come	them
Has	Name	Before	Her	Where	The

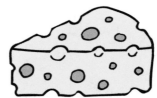

41

High-Flying Sentences

Color each flag that tells a complete thought.

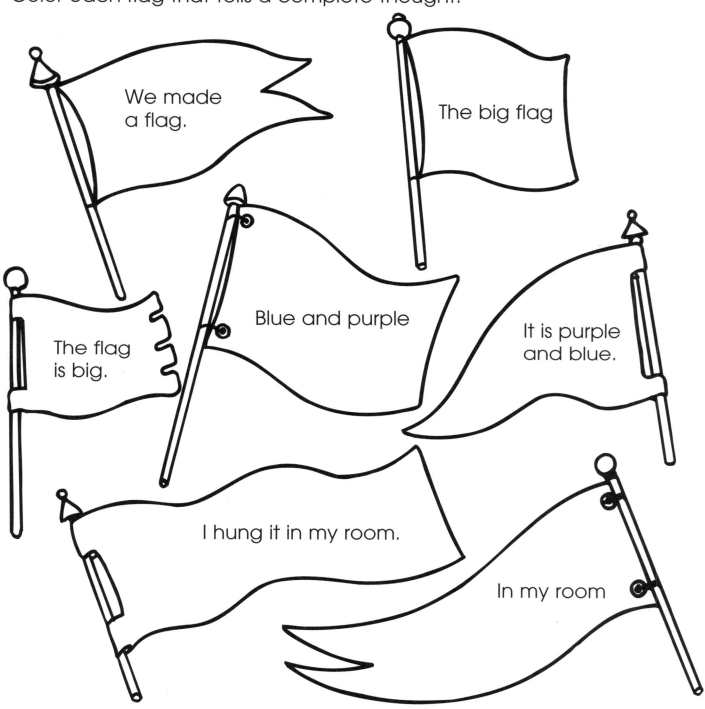

We made a flag.

The big flag

The flag is big.

Blue and purple

It is purple and blue.

I hung it in my room.

In my room

Scholastic Inc.   Summer Express: Between Grades K & 1

Months

January

February

March

April

May

June

Months

Trace and write.

July

August

September

October

November

December

Scholastic Inc.   Summer Express: Between Grades K & 1

Helping Your Child Get Ready: Week 4

These are the skills your child will be working on this week.

Math
- identifying 15 and 16
- identifying patterns

Reading and Phonics
- initial consonants
- sight words

Grammar
- capitalization

Here are some activities you and your child might enjoy.

Measuring with String Give your child a shoestring and have him or her look for objects that are longer than the string, then for objects that are shorter than the string.

Picture a Story Have your child search for an intriguing picture from a newspaper or magazine. Encourage him or her to tell a story about the picture. For example, if it's a picture of a whale breaching from the water, your child might say it's about a whale wanting to fly in the air.

Money Matters If you have a collection of loose coins, enlist your child's help in sorting, counting, and wrapping the coins to deposit in the bank.

Family Names Together with your child, write down the names of family members and friends. You can then count the number of letters in each name, or count the number of times a particular letter appears in the list of names and create a graph.

Your child might enjoy reading the following books:

Mr. Putter and Tabby Toot the Horn
by Cynthia Rylant

Song and Dance Man
by Karen Ackerman

Mary = 4

Tom = 3

Aisha = 5

Paolo = 5

_____ **'s Incentive Chart: Week 4**
Name Here

This week, I plan to read_____ minutes each day.

CHART YOUR PROGRESS HERE.

Week 4  I read for...	Day 1	Day 2	Day 3	Day 4	Day 5
	minutes	minutes	minutes	minutes	minutes
Put a sticker to show you completed each day's work.	◯ ◯	◯ ◯	◯ ◯	◯ ◯	◯ ◯

Congratulations!

Wow! You did a great job this week!

Place sticker here.

Parent or Caregiver's Signature_____

Fifteen Pennies

Trace and write.

1 5

Count the pennies in each bank. Color each bank with 15.

Scholastic Inc.   Summer Express: Between Grades K & 1

Sixteen Kites

Trace and write.

16 _____

Count the bows on each tail.
Color each kite with 16 bows.

Scholastic Inc.   Summer Express: Between Grades K & 1

What Comes Next?

Draw the shapes to complete each pattern.

1.

2.

3.

4. Draw a pattern using two shapes.

49

Button Patterns

Finish labeling each pattern.

1.

A   B   A   B   ___   ___

2.

A   A   B   A   ___   ___

3.

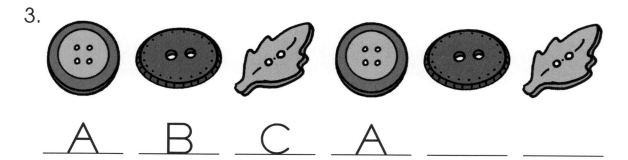

A   B   C   A   ___   ___

Look at each pattern. What kind of pattern is it? Circle the answer.

4.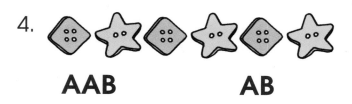

AAB   **AB**

5.

ABC   **ABB**

Hidden Letters

Say the name of each picture aloud. Look for the hidden letters that stand for the beginning sound of that name. Circle the hidden letters and then write the letters on the lines. Draw your own hidden letters picture in the empty box.

1.

_____
_____
_____

2.

_____
_____
_____

3.

_____
_____
_____

4.

_____
_____
_____

5.

_____
_____
_____

6.

_____
_____
_____

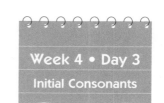

Show What You Know

Say the name of each picture. Fill in the circle next to the letter that stands for the missing sound. Write the letter on the line.

1.	○ d ○ b ○ y _____ uck	2.	○ q ○ x ○ p _____ ueen	3.	○ v ○ w ○ t _____ est
4.	○ b ○ p ○ h _____ at	5.	○ g ○ c ○ j _____ at	6.	○ p ○ f ○ d _____ ish
7.	○ l ○ k ○ h _____ ite	8.	○ x ○ z ○ y _____ ebra	9.	○ r ○ n ○ m _____ ope
10.	○ t ○ l ○ h _____ ape	11.	○ g ○ r ○ s _____ oat	12.	○ r ○ b ○ j _____ ike

Scholastic Inc. Summer Express: Between Grades K & 1

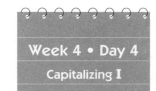
Capitalizing **I**

Always write the word **I** with a capital letter.

Read the sentences. Write **I** on the line.

1. _____ **will ride.**

2. _____ **will swim.**

3. **Mom and** _____ **will sing.**

4. **Then** _____ **will read.**

What will you do next? Write it on the line.

5. I will

Capitalize First Word

Read each sentence. Then fill in the circle next to the word with the capital letter that begins the sentence.

1. **The cat is in the van.**

    ◯ **cat**

    ◯ **The**

2. **My dog can run.**

    ◯ **My**

    ◯ **dog**

3. **Jan can hop.**

    ◯ **Jan**

    ◯ **hop**

4. **I like ham.**

    ◯ **ham**

    ◯ **I**

5. **Ants like jam.**

    ◯ **jam**

    ◯ **Ants**

Scholastic Inc. *Summer Express: Between Grades K & 1*

Write the Word *The*

Trace the word and say it aloud:

the   the   the

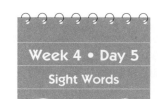

The sun is in the sky.

Write the word:

Write the word to finish the sentence:

___ ___ ___ sun is in the sky.

Write your own sentence using the word:

Cool Cat

Choose the word from the word bank that completes each sentence. Each word may be used only one time.

Word Bank

the	in
of	is
and	you
a	that
to	it

1. **Do you see ___ ___ ___ ___ cat?**

2. **The cat ___ ___ big and spotted.**

3. **That cat is next ___ ___   ___ ___ ___.**

4. **___ ___ is in a basket.**

5. **It is ___ ___   ___ basket with a pillow.**

6. **The cat ___ ___ ___ the basket are on top ___ ___ ___ ___ ___ bed.**

Write a sentence using some of the words from the word bank.

_____

_____

Scholastic Inc.   *Summer Express: Between Grades K & 1*

Helping Your Child Get Ready: Week 5

These are the skills your child will be working on this week.

Math
- identifying 17 and 18
- time

Reading and Phonics
- short vowels
- sight words

Grammar
- capitalization

Here are some activities you and your child might enjoy.

Shopping for Consonants While at the grocery store, pick a consonant letter and challenge your child to find and call out items that begin with that letter sound.

Graphing M&Ms Have your child graph the number of each color of M&Ms in a bag. You may want to give your child a sheet of graph paper on which to line up the M&Ms.

Fun With Fonts Let your child experiment on the computer with different fonts of the same letter.

Moon Mania Track the phases of the moon with your child for a month. (You don't have to go out every night.) Encourage your child to draw the shape of the moon each time you see it. After a few days, have your child predict what shape he or she will see the next night.

Your child might enjoy reading the following books:

Seven Blind Mice
by Ed Young

Cherries and Cherry Pits
by Vera B. Williams

_____ 's Incentive Chart: Week 5

Name Here

This week, I plan to read _____ minutes each day.

CHART YOUR PROGRESS HERE.

Week 5  I read for...	Day 1	Day 2	Day 3	Day 4	Day 5
	minutes	minutes	minutes	minutes	minutes
Put a sticker to show you completed each day's work.					

Congratulations!

Wow! You did a great job this week!

#1

Place sticker here.

Parent or Caregiver's Signature _____

Seventeen Gallons of Gas

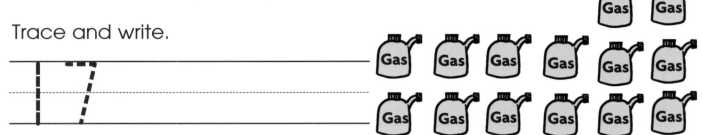

Trace and write.

17

Find the gas pump by following the numbers in order from 1 to 17.

Eighteen Stars

Trace and write.

18

Circle 18 stars in each picture.

Draw more stars to make 18.

Count the planets. Write the number. _____

Scholastic Inc.   Summer Express: Between Grades K & I

Get Tug's Mail

Tug the Bug wants to get his mail. To help him climb down the steps, say the name of each picture next to the boxes. Fill in the blank spaces with vowels to complete the words.

Calling All Words

Find the vowel sound that is missing from each word. Match the number in the word to the telephone code. Then write each word on the line.

1. c8p ___cup___

2. f2n _____

3. b4b _____

4. t3n _____

5. m6p _____

6. f6x _____

7. s2d _____

8. r3d _____

9. t8b _____

10. p4g _____

Squeak!

Circle the words that show the correct way to begin each sentence.

1. **The mouse**
    the mouse   is looking for food.

2. **he finds**
    He finds   a cracker on the floor.

3. **he Eats**
    He eats   the cracker.

4. **Then he**
    then He   takes a nap.

5. **oh No!**
    Oh no!   He hears a cat!

6. **the Mouse**
    The mouse   runs home fast!

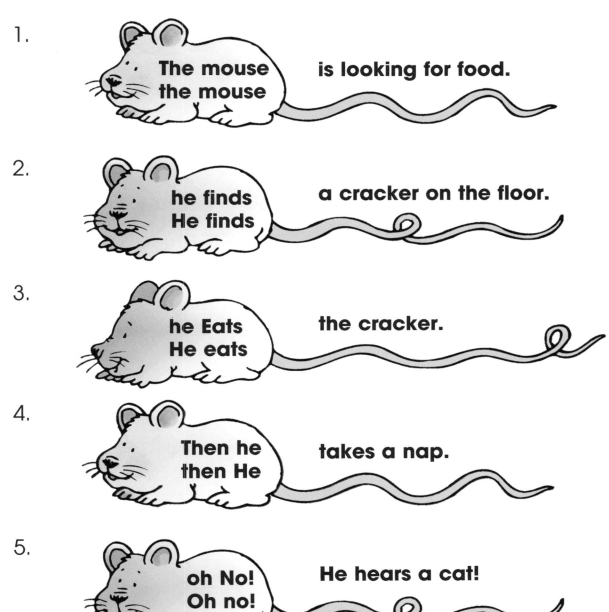

Sweet Dreams!

Write each beginning word correctly to make a sentence.

1.
my dog
_____
runs in her sleep.

2.
she must
_____
be dreaming.

3.
maybe she
_____
is chasing a cat.

4.
sometimes she
_____
even barks.

5.
i think
_____
it is funny.

Scholastic Inc. Summer Express: Between Grades K & 1

Write the Word *Have*

Trace the word and say it aloud:

have have

I **have** a new pet.

Write the word:

Write the word to finish the sentence:

I _____ a new pet.

Write your own sentence using the word:

My Bird Sam

Choose the word from the word bank that completes each sentence. Each word may be used only one time.

Word Bank

be	or
this	by
from	one
I	had
have	not

1. ___ had ___ ___ ___ bird. His name was Sam.

2. That is why I ___ ___ ___ ___   ___ ___ ___ ___ cage.

3. Sam ___ ___ ___ this cage.

4. He had come ___ ___ ___ ___ the pet store.

5. Sam could ___ ___ ___ sing ___ ___ talk.

6. He just liked to ___ ___   ___ ___ me.

Write a sentence using some of the words from the word bank.

_____

_____

Scholastic Inc. Summer Express: Between Grades K & 1

Telling Time

Write the time shown on each clock on the line.

1. ___ : ___ ___

2. ___ : ___ ___

3. ___ : ___ ___

4. ___ : ___ ___

5. ___ : ___ ___

6. ___ : ___ ___

7. ___ : ___ ___

8. ___ : ___ ___

9. Write the times in order from earliest to latest, starting at 1:00.

_____ , _____ , _____ , _____ , _____ , _____ , _____ , _____

10. Draw the hands on each clock to show the time you do each activity.

I get up each morning at

I eat dinner at

I eat breakfast at

I go to bed at

Half Past or Thirty Minutes

The time 12:30 can be read as twelve thirty or half past twelve. (One half hour is 30 minutes.) Write the correct time phrase from the box below under each clock.

Time Phrases	
half past 7	12:30
half past 2	5:30
half past 9	4:30
half past 1	3:30

Draw the hour and minute hands to show the time.

6:30

half past 8

Scholastic Inc. Summer Express: Between Grades K & I

Helping Your Child Get Ready: Week 6

These are the skills your child will be working on this week.

Math
- identifying 19 and 20
- measurement
- fractions

Reading and Phonics
- short vowels
- sight words

Grammar
- capitalization
- sentences

Here are some activities you and your child might enjoy.

"I Spy" a Rhyme Play an "I Spy" rhyming game with your child in your house or while walking around the neighborhood. For example, "I spy something that rhymes with *bee*." (*Tree*)

Bathtime Measurements Supply your child with measuring cups and spoons in the bathtub. Your child can explore how many tablespoons of water, for example, fit in one cup.

Order in the Kitchen Write a simple recipe (such as making instant pudding) on index cards, one direction per card. Read each step to your child. Then mix up the steps and ask your child to put the recipe back together in order. Then make the recipe with your child.

Word Search Look for a long word, such as *caterpillar*, and challenge your child to find shorter words within the word.

Your child might enjoy reading the following books:

Elizabeti's Doll
by Stephanie Stuve-Bodeen

The Secret Footprints
by Julia Alvarez

elephant

caterpillar

_____ **'s Incentive Chart: Week 6**

Name Here

This week, I plan to read_____ minutes each day.

CHART YOUR PROGRESS HERE.

Week 6  I read for...	Day 1	Day 2	Day 3	Day 4	Day 5
	minutes	minutes	minutes	minutes	minutes
Put a sticker to show you completed each day's work.					

Congratulations!

Wow! You did a great job this week!

Place sticker here.

Parent or Caregiver's Signature_____

Nineteen Marbles

Trace and write.

Circle the number that tells how many.
Color each group with 19 marbles.

17   18   19

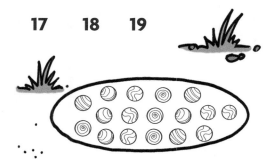

17   18   19

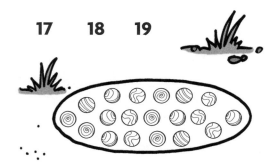

17   18   19

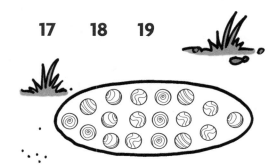

17   18   19

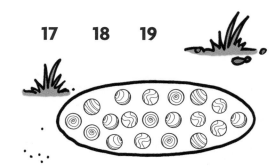

17   18   19

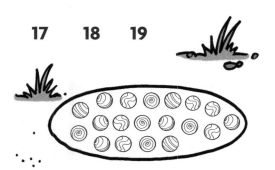

17   18   19

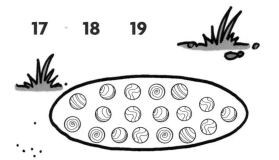

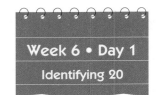
Twenty Butterflies to Count

Trace and write.

20

Write the numbers 1 to 20 on the trail.

Start

Find and color 20 butterflies in the picture.

Scholastic Inc.   *Summer Express: Between Grades K & 1*

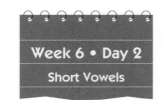

Short Vowel Crosswords

Use the picture clues to add a short vowel to each puzzle.

1.
W
P   N
G

2.
T
C   P
 B

3.
H
B   D
N

4.
T
F   X
P

5.
F
B   T
N

Show What You Know

Say the name of each picture. Fill in the circle next to the letter that stands for the missing sound. Write the letter on the line.

1. _____ ------------ c _____ t	○ a ○ e ○ i ○ o ○ u	2. _____ ------------ b _____ b	○ a ○ e ○ i ○ o ○ u	3. _____ ------------ b _____ d	○ a ○ e ○ i ○ o ○ u
4. _____ ------------ f _____ x	○ a ○ e ○ i ○ o ○ u	5. _____ ------------ b _____ g	○ a ○ e ○ i ○ o ○ u	6. _____ ------------ b _____ x	○ a ○ e ○ i ○ o ○ u
7. _____ ------------ _____ gg	○ a ○ e ○ i ○ o ○ u	8. _____ ------------ f _____ sh	○ a ○ e ○ i ○ o ○ u	9. _____ ------------ h _____ t	○ a ○ e ○ i ○ o ○ u

Scholastic Inc.   Summer Express: Between Grades K & 1

Counting Sheep

Write the beginning words correctly to make a sentence.

1.  we read
   _____
   _____
   _____ books before bed.

2.  then we
   _____
   _____
   _____ hug good night.

3.  my bed
   _____
   _____
   _____ is soft and cozy.

4.  my cat
   _____
   _____
   _____ sleeps with me.

5. the sky
   _____
   _____
   _____ has turned dark.

6.  my eyes
   _____
   _____
   _____ close.

Patriotic Sentences

Color the flag to show:

RED = sentence   WHITE = not a sentence

★ ★ ★ ★ ★ ★ ★ ★ ★ ★ ★ ★ ★ ★ ★ ★ ★ ★ ★ ★ ★ ★ ★ ★ ★ ★ ★ ★ ★ ★ ★ ★ ★ ★ ★ ★ ★ ★ ★ ★ ★ ★ ★ ★ ★ ★ ★ ★ ★ ★	**This is a flag.**
	The flag
	The flag has stars.
	The stars
	The stars are white.
	The stripes
	The stripes are red.

And white
The stripes are white.
Blue part
The flag has a blue part.
There are
There are 50 stars.

Scholastic Inc.   Summer Express: Between Grades K & 1

Write the Word *Was*

Trace the word and say it aloud:

was was was

This is me when *I **was** a baby.*

Write the word:

Write the word to finish the sentence:

This is me when I _____ a baby.

Write your own sentence using the word:

The Lost Bone

Choose the word from the word bank that completes each sentence. Each word may be used only one time.

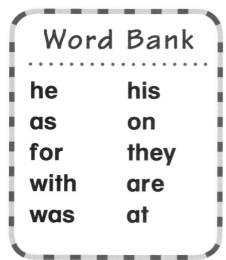

Word Bank

he	his
as	on
for	they
with	are
was	at

1. **This is Fred. ___ ___ is a dog.**

2. **Fred is as white ___ ___ snow.**

3. **He is ___ ___ ___ ___ ___ ___ ___ friend.**

4. **They ___ ___ ___ looking ___ ___ ___ a bone.**

5. **They look ___ ___ the tree and ___ ___ the grass.**

6. **___ ___ ___ ___ did not see the bone. It ___ ___ ___ gone.**

Write a sentence using some of the words from the word bank.

_____

_____

Scholastic Inc. Summer Express: Between Grades K & 1

Pencil Lengths

Cut out the apple ruler and use it to measure the pencils.
How many apples long is each pencil?

1. _____ apples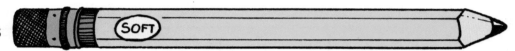

2. _____ apples

3. _____ apples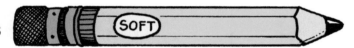

4. _____ apples

5. _____ apples

Fun With Fractions

A fraction is a part of a whole.

The shapes below are split into parts, or fractions.

Color only the shapes that are split into equal parts (equal fractions).

1.

2.

3.

4.

5.

6.

7.

8.

Scholastic Inc. Summer Express: Between Grades K & 1

Helping Your Child Get Ready: Week 7

These are the skills your child will be working on this week.

Math
- money
- patterns
- addition

Reading and Phonics
- rhyming words
- sight words

Writing and Grammar
- sentences

Here are some activities you and your child might enjoy.

Weighty Investigations Ask your child, "Do you think a cup of cotton balls weighs the same as a cup of paper clips?" Give your child two same-size paper cups and fill one with cotton balls and the other with paper clips. Have your child hold a cup in each hand and tell you which one is heavier. Encourage your child to think of other items to compare.

Blends and Digraphs As you and your child read a book, encourage your child to point out words that begin with consonant blends (two consonants together where the sound of each letter is heard, such as *gr*, *bl*, *sn*, and *tr*) or digraphs (two consonants that stand for one sound, such as *sh*, *ch*, *ph*, and *th*).

Rock Candy Make candy crystals with your child. Heat up 1/2 cup of water until it boils. Little by little, add one cup of sugar into the water until no more sugar will dissolve. When the liquid has cooled down a bit, carefully pour it into a glass. Put a Popsicle stick into the glass and set it aside in a place where it will be undisturbed. With your child, observe the glass and stick every day and watch as sugar crystals grow.

Magnetic Story Invite your child to create a short sentence, poem, or story on the refrigerator using magnetic words.

Your child might enjoy reading the following books:

The Squiggle
by Carole Lexa Schaefer

The Philharmonic Gets Dressed
by Karla Kuskin

Cookies Week
by Cindy Ward

_____'s Incentive Chart: Week 7

Name Here

This week, I plan to read _____ minutes each day.

CHART YOUR PROGRESS HERE.

Week 7	Day 1	Day 2	Day 3	Day 4	Day 5
I read for...	minutes	minutes	minutes	minutes	minutes
Put a sticker to show you completed each day's work.					

Congratulations!

Wow! You did a great job this week!

#1

Place sticker here.

Parent or Caregiver's Signature _____

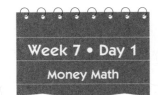

A Penny in Your Pocket

A penny equals 1¢. Count the pennies in each pocket.
Write the total.

1. 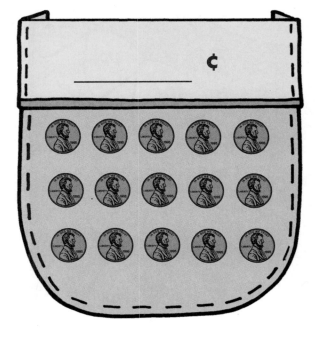 _____ ¢

2. 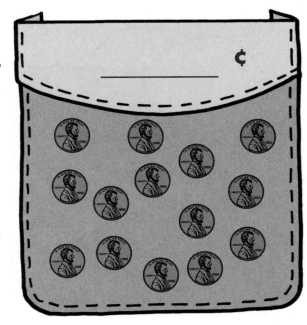 _____ ¢

3.  _____ ¢

4. 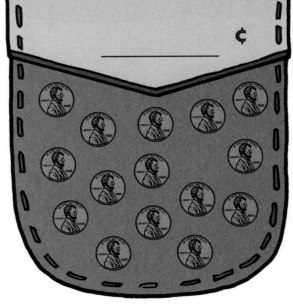 _____ ¢

The Tooth About Money

Look at Ali Gator's teeth.

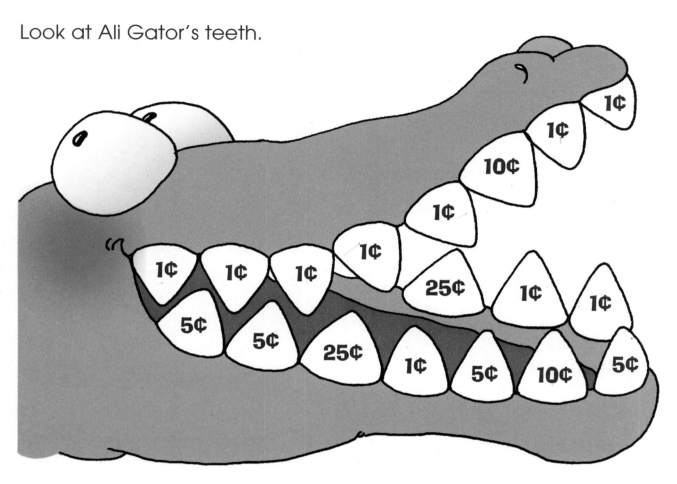

How many teeth?   How much money in all?

1. How many 1¢?   7   7   cents

2. How many 5¢?   4   20   cents

3. How many 10¢?   2   20   cents

4. How many 25¢?   2   50   cents

Scholastic Inc.   Summer Express: Between Grades K & 1

Hung Out to Dry

Cut out the pictures at the bottom. Paste them in place to continue each pattern.

Color or design these T-shirts in your own pattern.

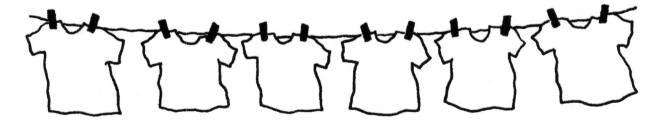

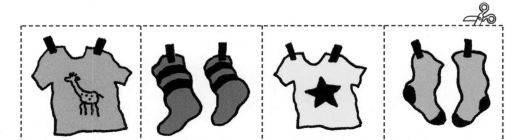

Scholastic Inc.   Summer Express: Between Grades K & 1

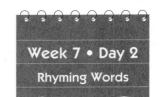

Show What You Know

Say the name of each picture. Fill in the circle next to the word that rhymes.

1. ○ big ◉ cat ○ bet	**2.** ◉ set ○ bat ○ new	**3.** ○ rip ◉ lap ○ can
4. ○ jet ○ jump ◉ hug	**5.** ◉ sink ○ wet ○ wing	**6.** ○ flag ○ vest ◉ fan
7. ○ best ◉ well ○ bit	**8.** ◉ dish ○ fit ○ fizz	**9.** ○ rip ◉ king ○ rest

Scholastic Inc.   Summer Express: Between Grades K & I

Write the Word *There*

Trace the word and say it aloud:

there   there

My dog is over **there.**

Write the word:

Write the word to finish the sentence:

My dog is over _____.

Write your own sentence using the word:

A Day at the Beach

Choose the word from the word bank that completes each sentence. Each word may be used only one time.

Word Bank

but	we
what	there
all	can
were	an
when	your

1. **We** ___ ___ ___ ___ **at the beach.**

2. ___ ___ ___ **of the fish were** ___ ___ ___ ___ ___ **.**

3. **We saw** ___ ___ **octopus** ___ ___ ___ **not a whale.**

4. ___ ___ **even saw a shark.**

5. **We saw** ___ ___ ___ ___ **favorite, a starfish!**

6. ___ ___ ___ ___ ___ ___ ___ ___ **you see**

   ___ ___ ___ ___ ___ **you go to the beach?**

Write a sentence using some of the words from the word bank.

_____

_____

Scholastic Inc. Summer Express: Between Grades K & 1

Mighty Good Sentences

Choose the ending that tells what each dog is doing. Remember to use periods.

is eating.

is sleeping.

is jumping.

is barking.

1. **The white dog** _____

   _____

2. **The gray dog** _____

   _____

3. **The spotted dog** _____

   _____

4. **The striped dog** _____

In the Rain Forest

Unscramble the words to make a sentence. Write the new sentence.
Do not forget to put a period at the end.

1. **A hiding jaguar is**

_____

- -

_____

2. **blue Some butterflies are**

_____

- -

3. **water in jump the Frogs**

_____

_____

4. **snakes trees Green hang from**

_____

- -

_____

5. **very tall grow The trees**

_____

- -

_____

Scholastic Inc.   Summer Express: Between Grades K & 1

Adding 1 to 5

Solve each problem.

1.

3 + 2 = _____

4.

2 + 1 = _____

2.

4 + 0 = _____

5.

1 + 3 = _____

3.

1 + 4 = _____

6.

5 + 0 = _____

7. Circle apples to show how many sets of 5 can you make.

I made _____ sets of 5.

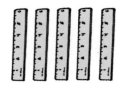

8. How many apples are left?

_____

Ways to Make 5

Cut out the pictures and arrange them to show the different ways of making 5. Glue the pictures down and write the addition sentences. Example:

1. + $1 + 4 = 5$

2. +  $3 + 2 = 5$

3. + $4 + 1 = 5$

4.  + $5 + 0 = 5$

5. +  $2 + 3 = 5$

Count the fingers.

6.  2

7.  5

Scholastic Inc. Summer Express: Between Grades K & 1

Helping Your Child Get Ready: Week 8

These are the skills your child will be working on this week.

Math
- counting
- data collection
- addition

Writing and Grammar
- punctuation

Reading and Phonics
- sight words
- word families

Here are some activities you and your child might enjoy.

Cereal Sorting After breakfast, engage your child in a sorting activity using multi-shaped, multi-colored cereal (such as Lucky Charms®). Invite your child to sort the cereal by shape or by color.

Riddle Me This Play a consonant riddle game with your child. Say a word, then challenge your child to find a rhyming word that starts with a given sound. For example, "What rhymes with *run* and starts with *f*?"

Menu Math While having dinner at a restaurant, encourage your child to explore the numbers on the price list. Ask questions such as, "How many items do you see that cost less than $10? What's the most expensive item on this menu? What's the least expensive item? How much do French fries cost?"

Funny Names Encourage your child to create a story starring a character with a silly rhyming or alliterative name, such as Funny Bunny, Matt the Cat, or Dilly Duck.

Your child might enjoy reading the following books:

Good Night, Good Knight
by Shelley Moore Thomas

The Bat Boy & His Violin
by Gavin Curtis

Inch by Inch
by Leo Lionni

_____
Name Here

's Incentive Chart: Week 8

This week, I plan to read_____ minutes each day.

CHART YOUR PROGRESS HERE.

Week 8  I read for...	Day 1	Day 2	Day 3	Day 4	Day 5
	minutes	minutes	minutes	minutes	minutes
Put a sticker to show you completed each day's work.					

Congratulations!

Wow! You did a great job this week!

Place sticker here.

Parent or Caregiver's Signature_____

Catch the Ball!

Count. Write how many.

Apples and Cores

Use the information shown below to answer the questions.

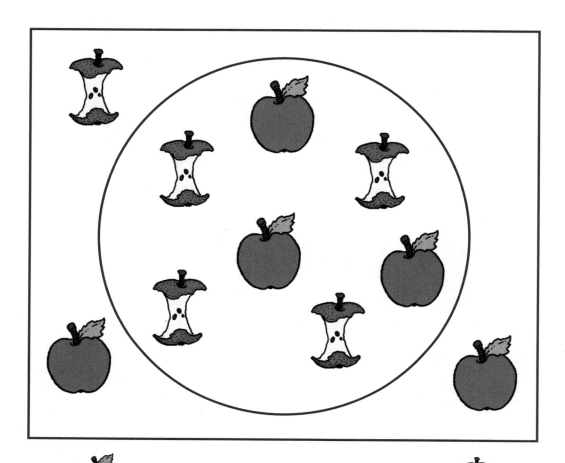

1. How many are in the circle? ___3___

2. How many are in the circle? ___4___

3. How many are not in the circle? ___2___

4. How many are not in the circle? ___1___

5. How many are there in all? ___5___

6. How many are there in all? ___5___

Scholastic Inc.   Summer Express: Between Grades K & 1

Periods

A telling sentence ends with a period.

Write a period where it belongs in each sentence. Read the sentences to a friend.

1. **Dan is in the cab**

2. **The cat is in the cab**

3. **Mom is in the cab**

4. **We see Dan and Mom**

Read the words. Write each word at the end of the correct sentence.

van.   red.

_____

- -

5. **We can go in the**_____

_____

- -

6. **The van is**_____

Twinkle, Twinkle Little Star

Rewrite each sentence using periods.

1. **Tonight I saw a star**
   _____
   _____

2. **I saw the star twinkle**
   _____
   _____

3. **It looked like a candle**
   _____
   _____

4. **It was very bright**
   _____
   _____

5. **I made a wish**
   _____
   _____

6. **I hope it comes true**
   _____
   _____

Telephone Math

What kind of phone never rings? _____

To find out, solve the addition problems. Then use the code on the telephone to replace your answers with letters. The first one has been done for you.

$$\begin{array}{r} 6 \\ + 2 \\ \hline 8 \end{array}$$ _A_

$$\begin{array}{r} 5 \\ + 1 \\ \hline \end{array}$$ _____

$$\begin{array}{r} 4 \\ + 4 \\ \hline \end{array}$$ _____

$$\begin{array}{r} 3 \\ + 6 \\ \hline \end{array}$$ _____

$$\begin{array}{r} 3 \\ + 0 \\ \hline \end{array}$$ _____

$$\begin{array}{r} 3 \\ + 4 \\ \hline \end{array}$$ _____

$$\begin{array}{r} 2 \\ + 2 \\ \hline \end{array}$$ _____

$$\begin{array}{r} 2 \\ + 1 \\ \hline \end{array}$$ _____

$$\begin{array}{r} 1 \\ + 1 \\ \hline \end{array}$$ _____

$$\begin{array}{r} 0 \\ + 1 \\ \hline \end{array}$$ _____

Write your telephone number in letters using the phone code above.

_____

Clowning Around

Add. Color the picture
using the color code.

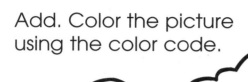

Color Code

1	pink
2	white
3	black
4	brown
5	purple
6	green
7	blue
8	orange
9	yellow
10	red

$5 + 2 =$

$\begin{array}{r} 4 \\ +5 \\ \hline \end{array}$

$\begin{array}{r} 5 \\ +0 \\ \hline \end{array}$

$6 + 3 =$

$\begin{array}{r} 2 \\ +3 \\ \hline \end{array}$

$\begin{array}{r} 7 \\ +2 \\ \hline \end{array}$

$\begin{array}{r} 4 \\ +4 \\ \hline \end{array}$

$2 + 5 =$

$3 + 2 =$

$\begin{array}{r} 4 \\ +3 \\ \hline \end{array}$

$\begin{array}{r} 3 \\ +3 \\ \hline \end{array}$

$\begin{array}{r} 1 \\ +0 \\ \hline \end{array}$

$\begin{array}{r} 4 \\ +2 \\ \hline \end{array}$

$\begin{array}{r} 0 \\ +1 \\ \hline \end{array}$

$\begin{array}{r} 5 \\ +1 \\ \hline \end{array}$

$4 + 1 =$

$\begin{array}{r} 6 \\ +2 \\ \hline \end{array}$

$\begin{array}{r} 2 \\ +1 \\ \hline \end{array}$

$7 + 0 =$

$\begin{array}{r} 3 \\ +0 \\ \hline \end{array}$

$\begin{array}{r} 3 \\ +5 \\ \hline \end{array}$

$5 + 5 =$

$6 + 1 =$

$\begin{array}{r} 1 \\ +1 \\ \hline \end{array}$

$7 + 3 =$

$3 + 1 =$

Scholastic Inc. Summer Express: Between Grades K & 1

Write the Word *Could*

Trace the word and say it aloud:

could could

I wanted to see if it **could** float. It can!

Write the word:

_____

- -

_____

Write the word to finish the sentence:

I wanted to see if it_____float.

Write your own sentence using the word:

_____

- -

_____

- -

_____

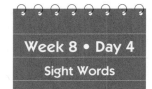

What a Watch!

Choose the word from the word bank that completes each sentence. Each word may be used only one time.

Word Bank

into	like
has	him
more	see
her	time
two	could

1. **Did you** ___ ___ ___ **the watch Jack put** ___ ___ ___ ___ **a box?**

2. **It looks** ___ ___ ___ ___ **like a car than a watch.**

3. **It** ___ ___ ___ ___ ___ ___ **hands and wheels.**

4. **It even tells the** ___ ___ ___ ___ **to** ___ ___ ___ **.**

5. **Maria would** ___ ___ ___ ___ **a watch like a car.**

6. **Jack** ___ ___ ___ ___ ___ **give it to** ___ ___ ___ **!**

Write a sentence using some of the words from the word bank.

_____

_____

Scholastic Inc. Summer Express: Between Grades K & 1

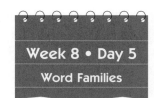

-at Family

Put the letters together to make the -at sound.

1. c + at = _____

2. b + at = _____

3. r + at = _____

4. h + at = _____

Look at the letters at the bottom of the page. Write them in the correct squares to finish each sentence.

5. Humpty Dumpty ☐at on a wall.

6. It was as ☐at as a pancake.

7. I like to ☐at on the telephone.

8. He coughed and ☐at out a gnat.

| fl | s | sp | ch |

Scholastic Inc.   Summer Express: Between Grades K & I

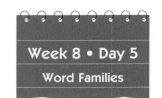
-in Family

Put the letters together to make the *-in* sound.

1. ch + in = _____

2. tw + in = _____

3. p + in = _____

4. f + in = _____

Look at the letters at the bottom of the page. Write them in the correct squares to finish each sentence.

5. Sam wants to ☐in the race.

6. Let's ☐in the top again.

7. The ball hit me on the ☐in.

8. A ☐in is a kind of smile.

| gr | sh | sp | w |

Scholastic Inc.   Summer Express: Between Grades K & 1

Helping Your Child Get Ready: Week 9

These are the skills your child will be working on this week.

Math
- counting
- measurement
- subtraction

Writing and Grammar
- punctuation
- sentences

Reading and Phonics
- initial consonants
- sight words
- word families

Here are some activities you and your child might enjoy.

Rhyming Pictures Give your child some old magazines and a pair of safety scissors. Then ask your child to cut out pictures of things whose names rhyme, such as *bat* and *hat*, or *coat* and *boat*.

Puzzling Sentences Write a sentence on a strip of paper, leaving lots of room between the words. For example, "Carlos is reading his favorite book." Cut the words apart and put them in an envelope. Have your child put together the words to form a sentence. (Notice that in some cases, children can form a statement as well as a question. For example, the above statement can also be changed to "Is Carlos reading his favorite book?")

Neighborhood Map While walking with your child, take pictures of different "landmarks" in your neighborhood, such as your own home, the grocery store, the mailbox, dry cleaners, playground, and so on. Then create a large map of the neighborhood with your child using the photographs to indicate different places.

Cereal Math Use candy or cereal to help introduce the concept of addition and subtraction to your child. For example, say, "If I have two pieces of cereal and you have one, how many do we both have?" Help your child count the total number of pieces.

Your child might enjoy reading the following books:

Dance, Tanya
by Satomi Ichikawa

Super Cluck
by Jane O'Connor

_____ 's Incentive Chart: Week 9

Name Here

This week, I plan to read _____ minutes each day.

CHART YOUR PROGRESS HERE.

Week 9  I read for...	Day 1	Day 2	Day 3	Day 4	Day 5
	minutes	minutes	minutes	minutes	minutes
Put a sticker to show you completed each day's work.	◯ ◯	◯ ◯	◯ ◯	◯ ◯	◯ ◯

Congratulations!

Wow! You did a great job this week!

Place sticker here.

Parent or Caregiver's Signature _____

Way to Go!

Count. Write how many.

_____

_____

_____

_____

_____

_____

Ribbon Lengths

Cut out the inch ruler and use it to measure the ribbons.
Write the length of each ribbon to the nearest inch.

1. _____ inches long

2. _____ inches long

3. _____ inches long

4. _____ inches long

5. _____ inch long

Glue the
other strip
here. Be
sure the end
meets this
line.

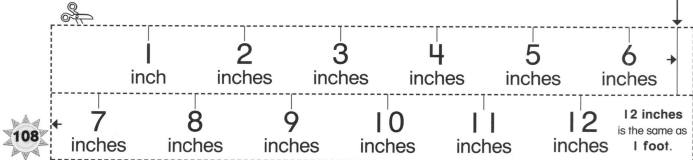

Scholastic Inc.   Summer Express: Between Grades K & 1

Periods

Read each group of words. Fill in the circle next to the correct sentence.

1.
- Ⓐ **The cat is on the mat.**
- Ⓑ **the cat is on the mat**
- Ⓒ **the cat on the mat**

2.
- Ⓐ **the rat is on the mop**
- Ⓑ **the rat is on the mop**
- Ⓒ **The rat is on the mop.**

3.
- Ⓐ **The rat sees the cat**
- Ⓑ **The rat sees the cat.**
- Ⓒ **the rat sees the cat**

4.
- Ⓐ **The rat can hop.**
- Ⓑ **The rat can hop**
- Ⓒ **the rat can hop**

5.
- Ⓐ **the cat and rat sit**
- Ⓑ **The cat and rat sit**
- Ⓒ **The cat and rat sit.**

Hop to It!

A telling sentence begins with a capital letter and ends with a period.
Rewrite each sentence correctly.

1. **frogs and toads lay eggs**

_____

_____

2. **the eggs are in the water**

_____

_____

3. **tadpoles hatch from the eggs**

_____

_____

4. **the tadpoles grow legs**

_____

_____

5. **the tadpoles lose their tails**

_____

_____

Scholastic Inc.   Summer Express: Between Grades K & 1

Scarecrow Subtraction

Cross out the pictures to solve each problem.

1.

$$6 - 4 = \underline{\qquad}$$

2.

$$5 - 3 = \underline{\qquad}$$

3.

$$6 - 1 = \underline{\qquad}$$

4. 4 crows are in the field.
The scarecrow scares 3 of the crows away.
How many crows are left?

$$4 - 3 = \underline{\qquad}$$

Juggling Act

Cross out. Write how many are left.

1. **3 – 1 =** _2_

2. **7 – 4 =** ____

3. **4 – 2 =** ____

4. **9 – 6 =** ____

5. **5 – 3 =** ____

6. **6 – 5 =** ____

Scholastic Inc. Summer Express: Between Grades K & 1

What's New?

Each bear has something new.

To find out what it is, say the name of each picture next to the bear. Listen for the beginning sound.

Write the letter that stands for that sound under the picture.

1.  ___ a ___

2.  ___ e ___ ___

3.  ___ o ___ ___ ___

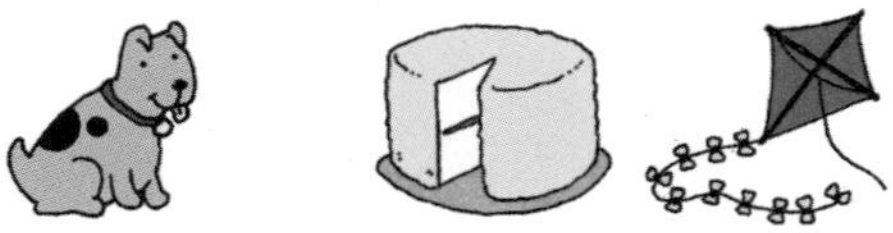

4.  ___ u ___ ___

5.  ___ ___ i ___ ___

Word Search

How many words can you find? Look for the words below and circle them.

a	n	b	e	b	i	g	f	o	r
n	a	l	o	i	s	v	u	n	m
d	p	u	g	g	o	t	n	m	a
w	q	e	b	c	n	h	l	k	k
e	r	d	c	h	e	r	j	s	e
c	f	e	i	i	h	e	i	e	u
r	u	n	t	u	p	e	s	e	t
d	o	w	n	a	m	a	k	o	n
l	w	e	r	t	o	p	m	y	t
y	o	u	m	p	l	a	y	a	m

am	at	blue	go	make	one	see	we
an	be	down	is	my	play	three	you
and	big	for	it	on	run	to	

Scholastic Inc.   Summer Express: Between Grades K & 1

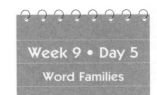

-ug Family

Put the letters together to make the *-ug* sound.

1. h + ug = _____

2. m + ug = _____

3. j + ug = _____

4. b + ug = _____

Look at the letters at the bottom of the page. Write them in the correct squares to finish each sentence.

5. I ☐ ug in the sand with a shovel.

6. Blankets keep us warm and ☐ ug.

7. He gave the string a ☐ ug.

8. Let's ☐ ug the hole.

| pl | d | sn | t |

-op Family

Put the letters together to make the *-op* sound.

1. t + **op** = _____

2. st + **op** = _____

3. m + **op** = _____

4. c + **op** = _____

Look at the letters at the bottom of the page. Write them in the correct squares to finish each sentence.

5. He can ☐op wood with an axe.

6. Let's ☐op like rabbits.

7. The farmer had a ☐op of corn.

8. We ☐op at the mall.

| cr | sh | h | ch |

Scholastic Inc.   Summer Express: Between Grades K & 1

Helping Your Child Get Ready: Week 10

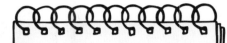

These are the skills your child will be working on this week.

Math
- counting
- estimation
- measurement
- addition
- subtraction

Reading and Phonics
- rhyming words
- word families
- sight words

Writing and Grammar
- sentences

Here are some activities you and your child might enjoy.

Digraph Search While flipping through a magazine, encourage your child to look for words with vowel digraphs (two vowels together that stand for one vowel sound, such as *ea*, *oo*, *oa*, and *ai*) and circle those words.

Making Words On a small chalkboard, write new words with phonograms. For example, starting with the word *cat*, erase the *c* and encourage your child to write a different consonant in its place to make a new word, such as *hat*, *bat*, or *mat*. Make sure all the words used are real.

Stargazing Take your child out on a clear, dark night to gaze at the stars. Point out familiar constellations, such as Orion or the Big Dipper. Then encourage your child to "connect the stars" to create his or her own patterns.

Counting Coins Give your child a collection of different coins. Ask your child to find different ways of making 50 cents or $1.

Your child might enjoy reading the following books:

Fox on Stage
by James Marshall

Mirandy and Brother Wind
by Patricia McKissack

_____ **'s Incentive Chart: Week 10**

Name Here

This week, I plan to read _____ minutes each day.

CHART YOUR PROGRESS HERE.

Week 10	Day 1	Day 2	Day 3	Day 4	Day 5
 I read for...	minutes	minutes	minutes	minutes	minutes
Put a sticker to show you completed each day's work.	○ ○	○ ○	○ ○	○ ○	○ ○

Congratulations!

Wow! You did a great job this week!

Place sticker here.

Parent or Caregiver's Signature _____

Out of This World

Count. Write how many. Color each group of 18 objects.

119

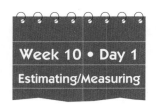
Look and Learn

Look at each picture. Estimate how long you think it is. Then measure each picture with a ruler. Write the actual length in inches.

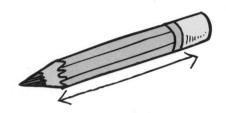

Estimate: _____ inches
Actual: _____ inches

Estimate: _____ inches
Actual: _____ inches

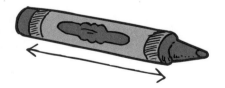

Estimate: _____ inches
Actual: _____ inches

Estimate: _____ inches
Actual: _____ inches

Practice measuring other things in the room with a ruler.

Scholastic Inc.   Summer Express: Between Grades K & 1

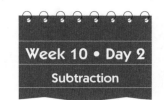
Trucking Along

Subtract. Color the picture using the color code.

Color Code

0	white
1	brown
2	black
3	green
4	purple
5	orange
6	yellow
7	blue
8	red

$9 - 2$

$7 - 6 =$

$9 - 1 =$

$8 - 4 =$

$7 - 3 =$

$6 - 2 =$

$10 - 6$

$9 - 5$

$4 - 4 =$

$5 - 2$

$1 - 1$

$10 - 7$

$10 - 4 =$

$10 - 2 =$

$8 - 2$

$10 - 9$

$6 - 3 =$

$9 - 7 =$

$9 - 4 =$

$9 - 3$

$10 - 8 =$

$7 - 5 =$

$9 - 6$

$8 - 2 =$

$4 - 3$

$9 - 1$

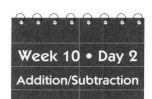

Blast Off

Add or subtract. Then use the code to answer the riddle below.

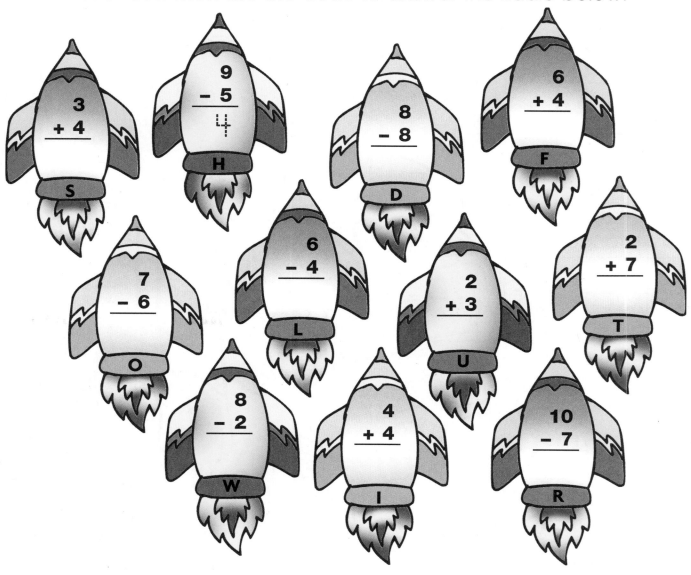

$3 + 4$ — S

$9 - 5 = 4$ — H

$8 - 8$ — D

$6 + 4$ — F

$7 - 6$ — O

$6 - 4$ — L

$2 + 3$ — U

$2 + 7$ — T

$8 - 2$ — W

$4 + 4$ — I

$10 - 7$ — R

How is an astronaut's job unlike any other job?

___ ___ ___ ' ___ ___ ___ ___ ___   ___ ___ ___
 8   9   7   1   5   9   1   10

___ H ___ ___   ___ ___ ___ ___ ___ ___ !
 9   4   8   7   6   1   3   2   0

Scholastic Inc.   Summer Express: Between Grades K & 1

Scat, Billy Bat!

Billy Bat is lost in the city. Help him get home to his cave. Follow the streets whose names rhyme with *bat* to find the way.

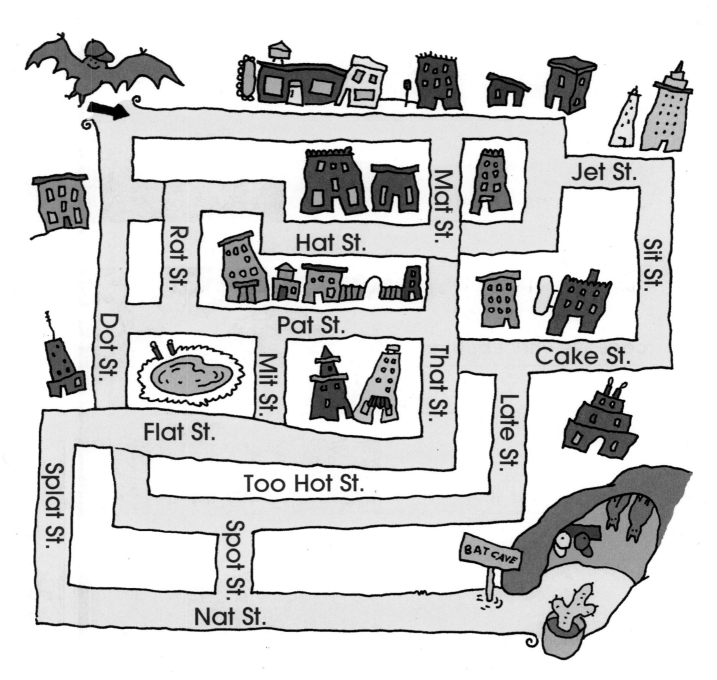

Hop to It Some More!

Rewrite each sentence. Use capital letters and periods correctly.

1. **tadpoles become frogs or toads**

_____

_____

2. **frogs live near water**

_____

_____

3. **toads live under bushes**

_____

_____

4. **frogs have wet skin**

_____

_____

5. **toads have bumpy skin**

_____

_____

Scholastic Inc.   Summer Express: Between Grades K & I

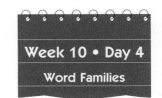

-est Family

Put the letters together to make the *-est* sound.

1. v + **est** = _____

2. n + **est** = _____

3. ch + **est** = _____

4. p + **est** = _____

Look at the letters at the bottom of the page. Write them in the correct squares to finish each sentence.

5. He is tired. He needs to ☐est.

6. Do your ☐est work.

7. Travel east, not ☐est.

8. I'm ready to take the ☐est.

| b | r | w | t |

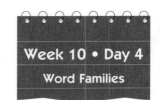

-ock Family

Put the letters together to make the -ock sound.

1. r + ock = _____

2. s + ock = _____

3. cl + ock = _____

4. d + ock = _____

Look at the letters at the bottom of the page. Write them in the correct squares to finish each sentence.

5. Put on a ☐ock before you paint.

6. A ☐ock of geese flew south.

7. Did you hear a ☐ock at the door?

8. We need to ☐ock the gate.

| l | kn | fl | sm |

Scholastic Inc.   Summer Express: Between Grades K & 1

The Continents

Write the names of the continents.

Africa _____

_____

_____

Asia _____

_____

_____

Australia _____

_____

_____

Antarctica _____

_____

_____

Europe _____

_____

_____

North America _____

_____

_____

South America _____

_____

_____

Africa

Asia

Antarctica

Australia

Europe

North America

South America

Scholastic Inc.   Summer Express: Between Grades K & I

127

Word Search

How many words can you find? Look for the words below and circle them.

t	l	r	q	p	c	d	i	d	a
h	h	i	j	k	a	y	m	n	e
e	a	t	f	g	m	z	o	f	v
r	s	h	a	v	e	d	u	o	v
e	t	e	e	d	c	c	n	u	w
u	p	y	e	s	b	a	d	r	g
v	l	b	w	o	u	t	e	d	v
w	e	x	h	o	y	z	r	i	h
r	a	q	i	n	o	w	b	n	i
o	s	p	t	c	u	k	j	t	u
n	e	m	e	l	r	s	t	o	a

came	four	into	now	please	under	white
did	have	it	on	soon	up	yes
eat	in	me	out	there	we	

Scholastic Inc.   Summer Express: Between Grades K & 1

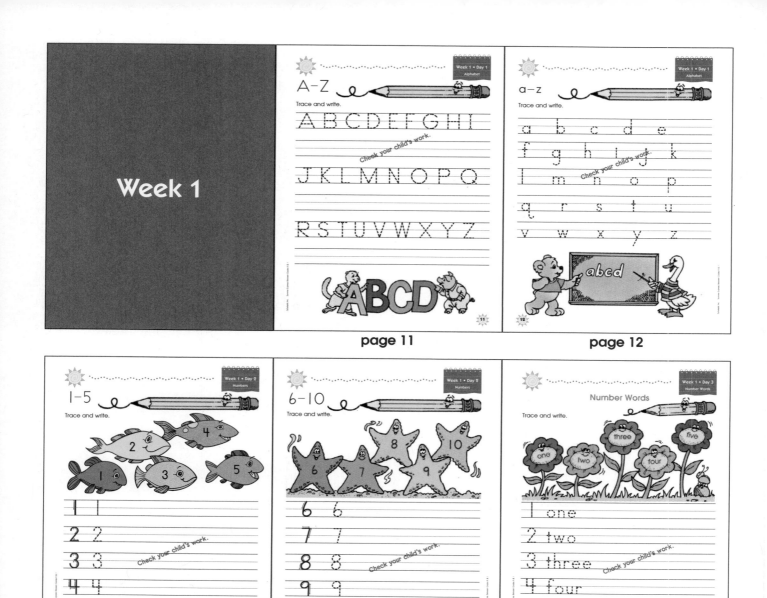

page 11

page 12

Week 1

A–Z
Trace and write.
Week 1 • Day 1
Alphabet
A B C D E F G H I
J K L M N O P Q
R S T U V W X Y Z

a–z
Trace and write.
Week 1 • Day 1
Alphabet
a b c d e
f g h i j k
l m n o p
q r s t u
v w x y z

1–5
Trace and write.
Week 1 • Day 2
Numbers
1 1
2 2
3 3
4 4
5 5

6–10
Trace and write.
Week 1 • Day 2
Numbers
6 6
7 7
8 8
9 9
10 10

Number Words
Trace and write.
Week 1 • Day 3
Number Words
1 one
2 two
3 three
4 four
5 five

page 13

page 14

page 15

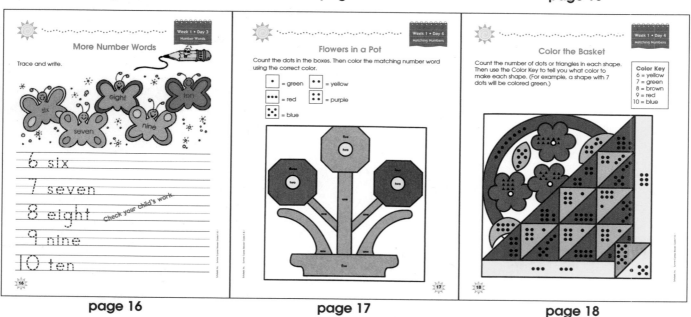

More Number Words
Trace and write.
Week 1 • Day 3
Number Words
6 six
7 seven
8 eight
9 nine
10 ten

Flowers in a Pot
Week 1 • Day 4
Matching Numbers
Count the dots in the boxes. Then color the matching number word using the correct color.
= green
= yellow
= red
= purple
= blue

Color the Basket
Week 1 • Day 4
Matching Numbers
Count the number of dots or triangles in each shape. Then use the Color Key to tell you what color to make each shape. (For example, a shape with 7 dots will be colored green.)
Color Key
6 = yellow
7 = green
8 = brown
9 = red
10 = blue

page 16

page 17

page 18

Color Words

Trace and write.

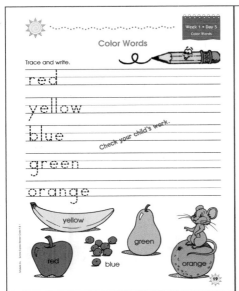

red

yellow

blue

green

orange

Check your child's work.

More Color Words

Trace and write.

purple

brown

black

white

pink

Check your child's work.

pink purple white brown black

page 19   **page 20**

Week 2

Eleven Excited Earthworms

Trace and write.

11 *Check your child's work.*

Color each set of 11 earthworms.

Twelve Tasty Treats

Trace and write.

12 *Check your child's work.*

Count the candy in each jar. Color each jar with 12.

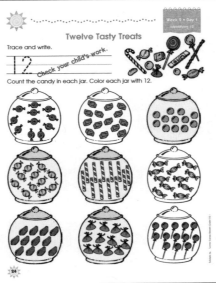

Number User

I use numbers to tell about myself.

1. _____
   My   Street Number

2. _____
   My   Zip Code

3. _____
   My   Telephone Number

4. _____
   My   Birthday

5. _____
   My   Age

6. _____
   My   Height and Weight

7. _____
      Number of People in My Family

   I can count up to

8. _____

Check your child's work.

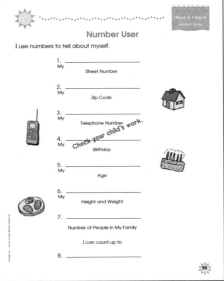

page 23   **page 24**   **page 25**

Sign Shape

Street signs come in different shapes. Answer the questions below about the shapes.

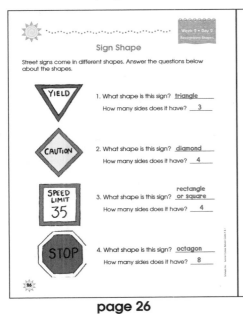

1. What shape is this sign? __triangle__

   How many sides does it have? __3__

2. What shape is this sign? __diamond__

   How many sides does it have? __4__

3. What shape is this sign? __rectangle or square__

   How many sides does it have? __4__

4. What shape is this sign? __octagon__

   How many sides does it have? __8__

Food Puzzles

Say the name of each food. Find the letter that stands for the beginning sound of each food. Draw a line from each food to its beginning letter sound.

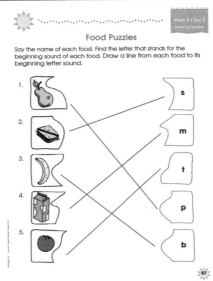

1.   s
2.   m
3.   t
4.   p
5.   b

Whose Toy Is It?

Read the names on the children's T-shirts aloud. Each child plays only with toys whose names begin with the same sound as his or her name. Fill in the letter that each toy begins with. Then draw lines from each child to the matching toys.

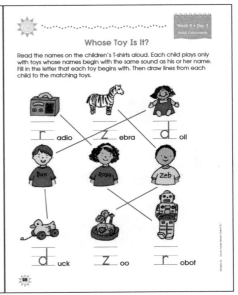

r adio   z ebra   d oll

Dan   Rosa   Zeb

d uck   z oo   r obot

page 26   **page 27**   **page 28**

What's Missing?

Look at each set of pictures below. What is missing from the pictures on the right side? Draw what's missing to make both pictures the same.

Check your child's work.

page 29

What's Different?

Look at the top and bottom pictures. Are they exactly the same? Color the three things you see in the bottom picture that are not in the top picture.

Check your child's work.

page 30

Shapes

Trace and write.

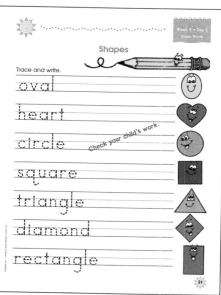

oval

heart

circle   *Check your child's work.*

square

triangle

diamond

rectangle

page 31

Days of the Week

Trace and write.

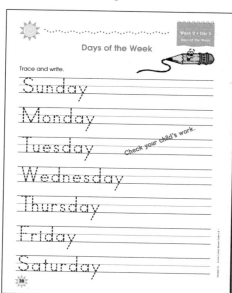

Sunday

Monday

Tuesday   *Check your child's work.*

Wednesday

Thursday

Friday

Saturday

page 32

Week 3

Thirteen Tasty Bones

Trace and write.

13   *Check your child's work.*

Circle 13 bones in each picture.

Draw more bones to make 13.

Count the bones. Circle the correct number.   12 (13) 14

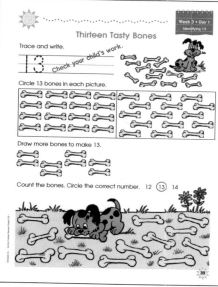

page 35

Juggling Fourteen Balls

Trace and write.

14   *Check your child's work.*

Color each ball with 14 dots.

page 36

Face First

The pictures show animal faces. Can you name each animal? Write the letter that each animal's name begins with.

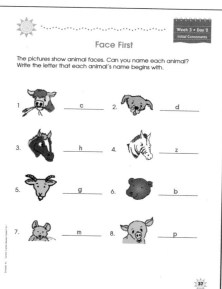

1. c
2. d
3. h
4. z
5. g
6. b
7. m
8. p

page 37

What's That Sound?

Say the name of each picture aloud. Choose the letter from the box that stands for the beginning sound of the name. Write it on the line in the speech bubble.

Bb Pp Rr Ww Yy Zz

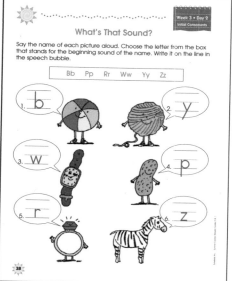

1. b
2. y
3. W
4. p
5. r
6. z

page 38

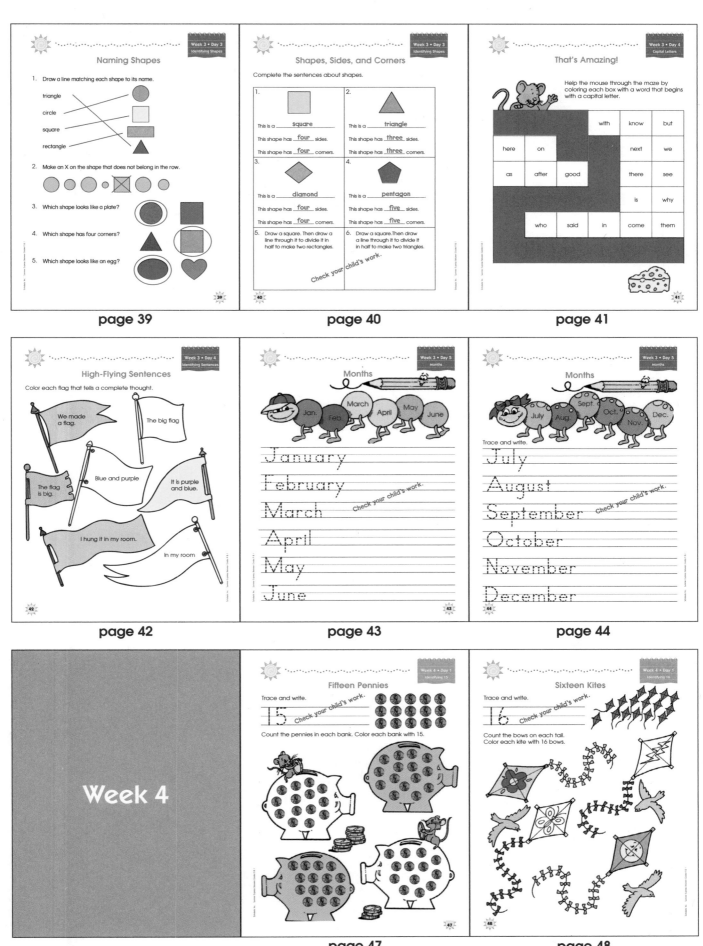

page 39

Naming Shapes

1. Draw a line matching each shape to its name.

triangle
circle
square
rectangle

2. Make an X on the shape that does not belong in the row.

3. Which shape looks like a plate?

4. Which shape has four corners?

5. Which shape looks like an egg?

page 40

Shapes, Sides, and Corners

Complete the sentences about shapes.

1. This is a __square__
This shape has __four__ sides.
This shape has __four__ corners.

2. This is a __triangle__
This shape has __three__ sides.
This shape has __three__ corners.

3. This is a __diamond__
This shape has __four__ sides.
This shape has __four__ corners.

4. This is a __pentagon__
This shape has __five__ sides.
This shape has __five__ corners.

5. Draw a square. Then draw a line through it to divide it in half to make two rectangles.

6. Draw a square. Then draw a line through it to divide it in half to make two triangles.

Check your child's work.

page 41

That's Amazing!

Help the mouse through the maze by coloring each box with a word that begins with a capital letter.

			with	know	but
here	on			next	we
as	after	good		there	see
				is	why
who	said	in	come	them

page 42

High-Flying Sentences

Color each flag that tells a complete thought.

We made a flag.

The big flag

The flag is big.

Blue and purple

It is purple and blue.

I hung it in my room.

In my room

page 43

Months

January
February
March
April
May
June

Check your child's work.

page 44

Months

Trace and write.

July
August
September
October
November
December

Check your child's work.

Week 4

page 47

Fifteen Pennies

Trace and write.

15 *Check your child's work.*

Count the pennies in each bank. Color each bank with 15.

page 48

Sixteen Kites

Trace and write.

16 *Check your child's work.*

Count the bows on each tail. Color each kite with 16 bows.

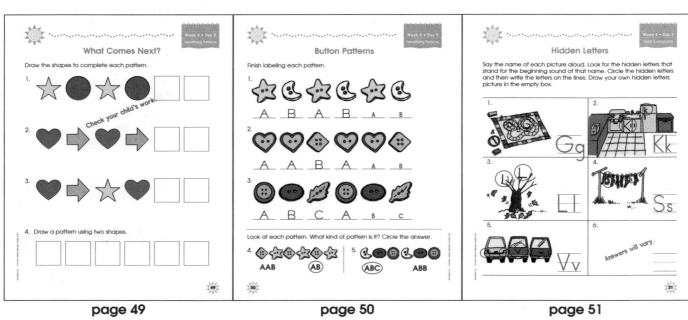

page 49
          page 50
          page 51

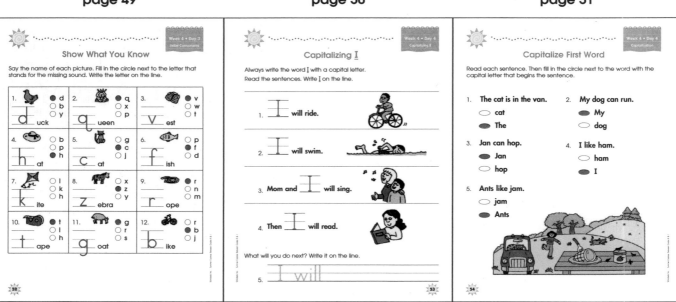

page 52
          page 53
          page 54

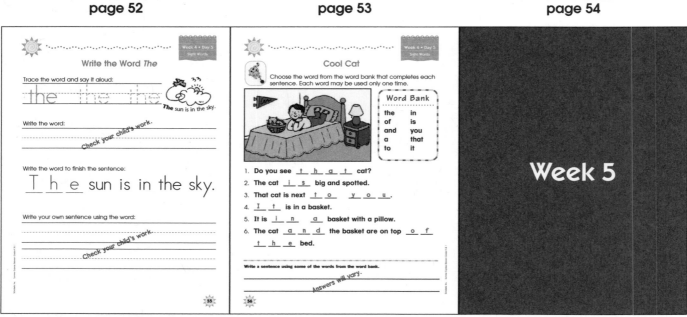

page 55
          page 56

Seventeen Gallons of Gas

Trace and write.

Check your child's work.

Find the gas pump by following the numbers in order from 1 to 17.

page 59

Eighteen Stars

Trace and write.

Check your child's work.

Circle 18 stars in each picture.

Draw more stars to make 18.

Count the planets. Write the number. __18__

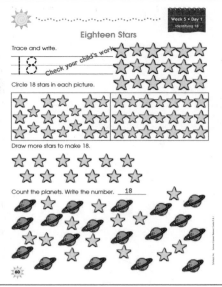

page 60

Get Tug's Mail

Tug the Bug wants to get his mail. To help him climb down the steps, say the name of each picture next to the boxes. Fill in the blank spaces with vowels to complete the words.

c a t
  o
p i n
  u t
t u b
  e
  d

page 61

Calling All Words

Find the vowel sound that is missing from each word. Match the number in the word to the telephone code. Then write each word on the line.

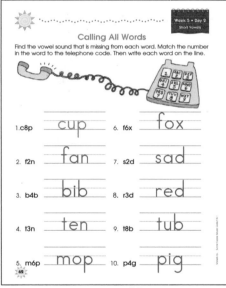

1. c8p   cup
2. f2n   fan
3. b4b   bib
4. t3n   ten
5. m6p   mop

6. f6x   fox
7. s2d   sad
8. r3d   red
9. t8b   tub
10. p4g   pig

page 62

Squeak!

Circle the words that show the correct way to begin each sentence.

1. (The mouse) / the mouse — is looking for food.
2. he finds / (He finds) — a cracker on the floor.
3. he Eats / (He eats) — the cracker.
4. (Then he) / then He — takes a nap.
5. (Oh No!) / Oh no! — He hears a cat!
6. the Mouse / (The mouse) — runs home fast!

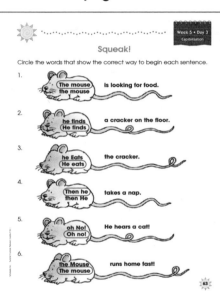

page 63

Sweet Dreams!

Write each beginning word correctly to make a sentence.

1. my dog — My dog — runs in her sleep.
2. she must — She must — be dreaming.
3. maybe she — Maybe she — is chasing a cat.
4. sometimes she — Sometimes she — even barks.
5. i think — I think — it is funny.

page 64

Write the Word *Have*

Trace the word and say it aloud:

have have

I **have** a new pet.

Write the word:

Check your child's work.

Write the word to finish the sentence:

I h a v e a new pet.

Write your own sentence using the word:

Check your child's work.

page 65

My Bird Sam

Choose the word from the word bank that completes each sentence. Each word may be used only one time.

Word Bank	
be	or
this	by
from	one
I	had
have	not

1. I had o n e bird. His name was Sam.
2. That is why I h a v e t h i s cage.
3. Sam h a d this cage.
4. He had come f r o m the pet store.
5. Sam could n o t sing o r talk.
6. He just liked to b e b y me.

Write a sentence using some of the words from the word bank.

Answers will vary.

page 66

Telling Time

Write the time shown on each clock on the line.

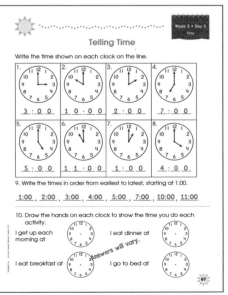

1. 3:00
2. 10:00
3. 2:00
4. 7:00
5. 5:00
6. 11:00
7. 1:00
8. 4:00

9. Write the times in order from earliest to latest, starting at 1:00.

1:00 2:00 3:00 4:00 5:00 7:00 10:00 11:00

10. Draw the hands on each clock to show the time you do each activity.

I get up each morning at

I eat dinner at

I eat breakfast at

I go to bed at

Answers will vary.

page 67

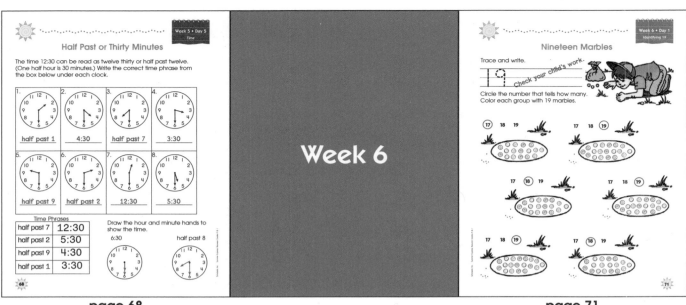

page 68

page 71

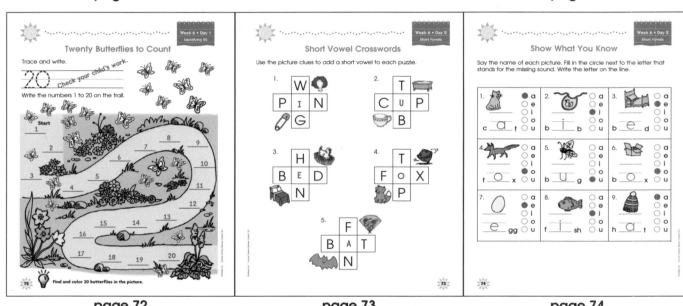

page 72

page 73

page 74

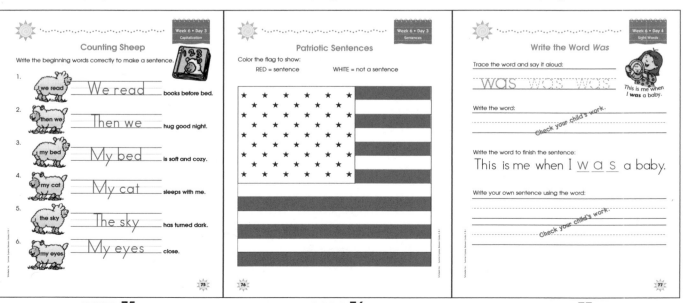

page 75

page 76

page 77

The Lost Bone

Choose the word from the word bank that completes each sentence. Each word may be used only one time.

Word Bank

he	his
as	on
for	they
with	are
was	at

1. This is Fred. _H e_ is a dog.
2. Fred is as white _a s_ snow.
3. He is _w i t h   h i s_ friend.
4. They _a r e_ looking _f o r_ a bone.
5. They look _a t_ the tree and _o n_ the grass.
6. _T h e y_ did not see the bone. It _w a s_ gone.

Write a sentence using some of the words from the word bank.

Answers will vary.

page 78

Pencil Lengths

Cut out the apple ruler and use it to measure the pencils. How many apples long is each pencil?

1. _6_ apples
2. _2_ apples
3. _4_ apples
4. _3_ apples
5. _5_ apples

page 79

Fun With Fractions

A fraction is a part of a whole.
The shapes below are split into parts, or fractions.
Color only the shapes that are split into equal parts (equal fractions).

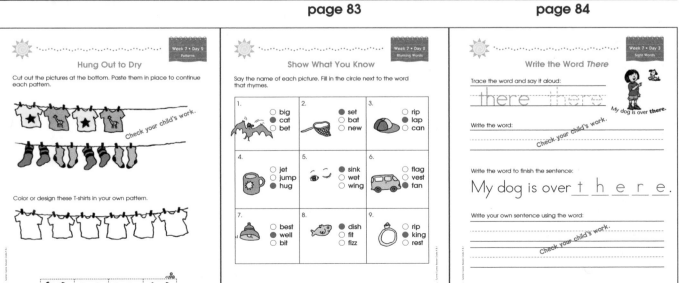

page 80

Week 7

A Penny in Your Pocket

A penny equals 1¢. Count the pennies in each pocket. Write the total.

1. _15_ ¢
2. _14_ ¢
3. _13_ ¢
4. _15_ ¢

page 83

The Tooth About Money

Look at Ali Gator's teeth.

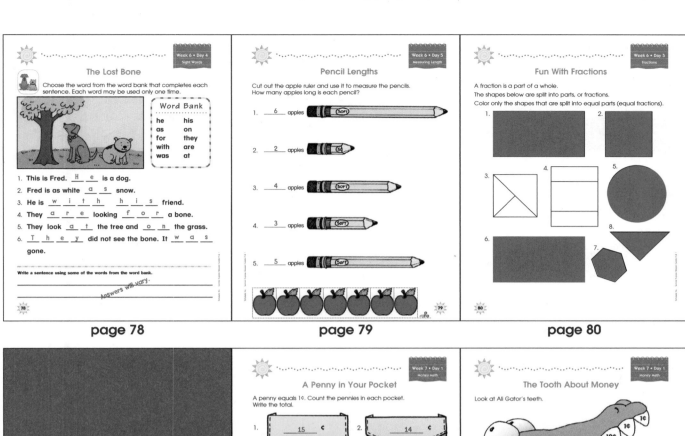

How many teeth? How much money in all?

1. How many 1¢? _10_ | _10_ cents
2. How many 5¢? _4_ | _20_ cents
3. How many 10¢? _2_ | _20_ cents
4. How many 25¢? _2_ | _50_ cents

page 84

Hung Out to Dry

Cut out the pictures at the bottom. Paste them in place to continue each pattern.

Check your child's work.

Color or design these T-shirts in your own pattern.

page 85

Show What You Know

Say the name of each picture. Fill in the circle next to the word that rhymes.

1. ○ big ● cat ○ bet	2. ● set ○ bat ○ new	3. ○ rip ● lap ○ can
4. ○ jet ○ jump ● hug	5. ● sink ○ wet ○ wing	6. ○ flag ○ vest ● fan
7. ○ best ● well ○ bit	8. ● dish ○ fit ○ fizz	9. ○ rip ● king ○ rest

page 86

Write the Word *There*

Trace the word and say it aloud:

there there

My dog is over **there.**

Write the word:

Check your child's work.

Write the word to finish the sentence:

My dog is over _t h e r e_.

Write your own sentence using the word:

Check your child's work.

page 87

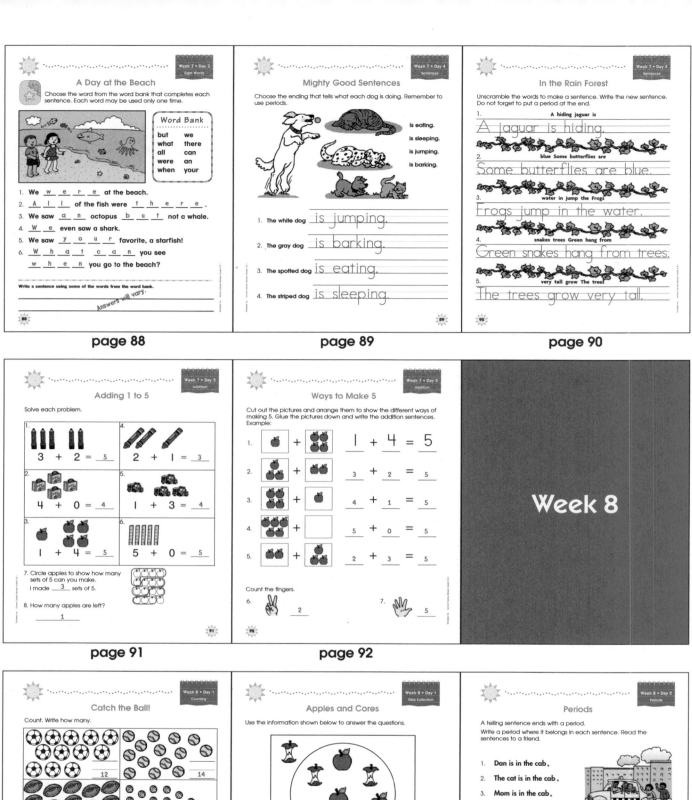

page 88

page 89

page 90

page 91

page 92

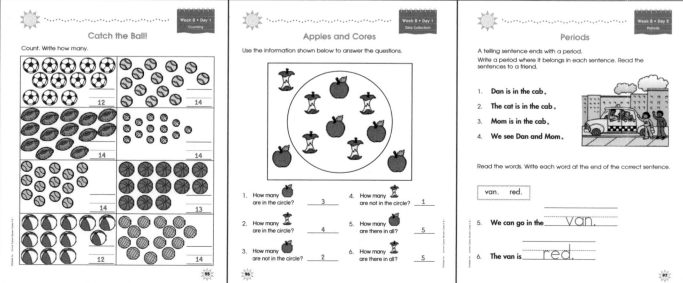

page 95

page 96

page 97

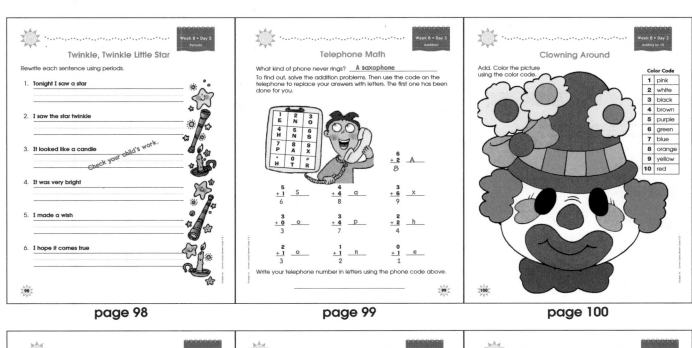

page 98

Twinkle, Twinkle Little Star

Rewrite each sentence using periods.

1. Tonight I saw a star

2. I saw the star twinkle

3. It looked like a candle

4. It was very bright

5. I made a wish

6. I hope it comes true

Check your child's work.

page 99

Telephone Math

What kind of phone never rings? __A saxophone__

To find out, solve the addition problems. Then use the code on the telephone to replace your answers with letters. The first one has been done for you.

$$6 + 2 = 8 \quad A$$

$$5 + 1 = 6 \quad S$$
$$4 + 4 = 8 \quad a$$
$$3 + 6 = 9 \quad x$$

$$3 + 0 = 3 \quad o$$
$$3 + 4 = 7 \quad p$$
$$2 + 2 = 4 \quad h$$

$$2 + 1 = 3 \quad o$$
$$1 + 1 = 2 \quad n$$
$$0 + 1 = 1 \quad e$$

Write your telephone number in letters using the phone code above.

page 100

Clowning Around

Add. Color the picture using the color code.

Color Code	
1	pink
2	white
3	black
4	brown
5	purple
6	green
7	blue
8	orange
9	yellow
10	red

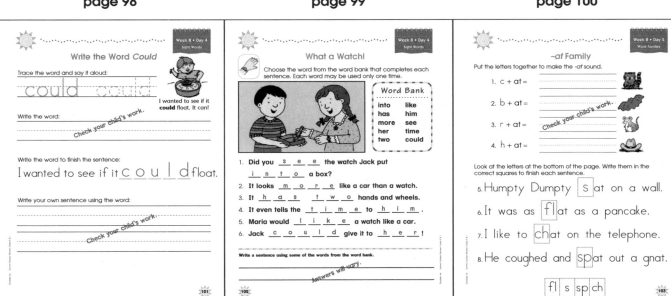

page 101

Write the Word *Could*

Trace the word and say it aloud:

could   could

I wanted to see if it could float. It can!

Write the word:

Check your child's work.

Write the word to finish the sentence:

I wanted to see if it C O U L D float.

Write your own sentence using the word:

Check your child's work.

page 102

What a Watch!

Choose the word from the word bank that completes each sentence. Each word may be used only one time.

Word Bank	
into	like
has	him
more	see
her	time
two	could

1. Did you _s e e_ the watch Jack put _i n t o_ a box?
2. It looks _m o r e_ like a car than a watch.
3. It _h a s_ _t w o_ hands and wheels.
4. It even tells the _t i m e_ to _h i m_.
5. Maria would _l i k e_ a watch like a car.
6. Jack _c o u l d_ give it to _h e r_!

Write a sentence using some of the words from the word bank.

Answers will vary.

page 103

-at Family

Put the letters together to make the -at sound.

1. c + at =
2. b + at =
3. r + at =
4. h + at =

Check your child's work.

Look at the letters at the bottom of the page. Write them in the correct squares to finish each sentence.

5. Humpty Dumpty [S] at on a wall.
6. It was as [fl] at as a pancake.
7. I like to [ch] at on the telephone.
8. He coughed and [sp] at out a gnat.

[fl] [s] [sp] [ch]

page 104

-in Family

Put the letters together to make the -in sound.

1. ch + in =
2. tw + in =
3. p + in =
4. f + in =

Check your child's work.

Look at the letters at the bottom of the page. Write them in the correct squares to finish each sentence.

5. Sam wants to [W] in the race.
6. Let's [sp] in the top again.
7. The ball hit me on the [sh] in.
8. A [gr] in is a kind of smile.

[gr] [sh] [sp] [w]

Week 9

page 107

Way to Go!

Count. Write how many.

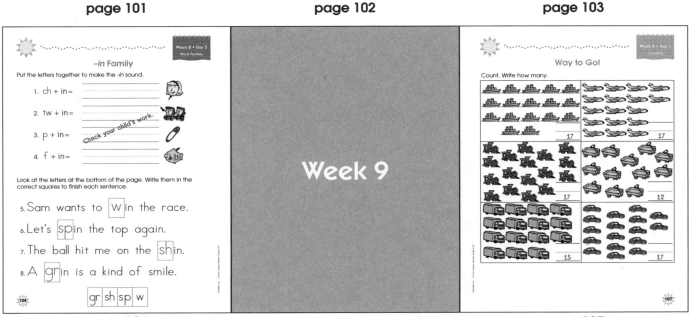

17   17

17   12

15   17

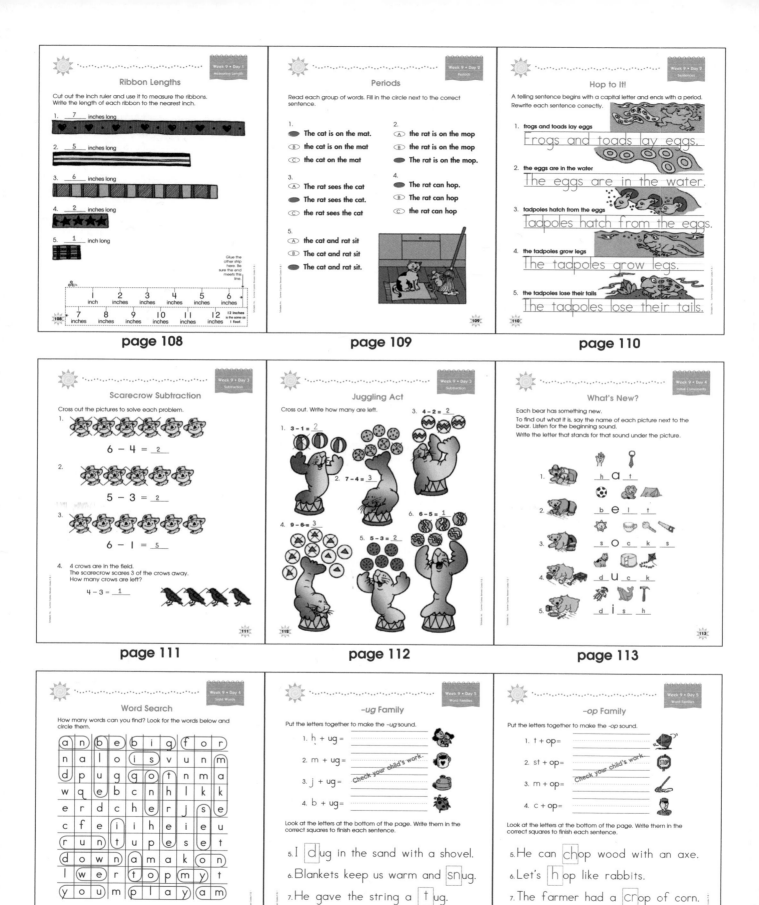

page 108

Ribbon Lengths

Cut out the inch ruler and use it to measure the ribbons.
Write the length of each ribbon to the nearest inch.

1. 7 inches long
2. 5 inches long
3. 6 inches long
4. 2 inches long
5. 1 inch long

Glue the other strip here. Be sure the end meets this line.

| 1 inch | 2 inches | 3 inches | 4 inches | 5 inches | 6 inches |
| 7 inches | 8 inches | 9 inches | 10 inches | 11 inches | 12 inches |

12 inches is the same as 1 foot.

Week 9 • Day 1
Measuring Length

---

page 109

Periods

Read each group of words. Fill in the circle next to the correct sentence.

1.
● The cat is on the mat.
Ⓑ the cat is on the mat
Ⓒ the cat on the mat

2.
Ⓐ the rat is on the mop
Ⓑ the rat is on the mop
● The rat is on the mop.

3.
Ⓐ The rat sees the cat
● The rat sees the cat.
Ⓒ the rat sees the cat

4.
● The rat can hop.
Ⓑ The rat can hop
Ⓒ the rat can hop

5.
Ⓐ the cat and rat sit
Ⓑ The cat and rat sit
● The cat and rat sit.

Week 9 • Day 2
Periods

---

page 110

Hop to It!

A telling sentence begins with a capital letter and ends with a period.
Rewrite each sentence correctly.

1. frogs and toads lay eggs

Frogs and toads lay eggs.

2. the eggs are in the water

The eggs are in the water.

3. tadpoles hatch from the eggs

Tadpoles hatch from the eggs.

4. the tadpoles grow legs

The tadpoles grow legs.

5. the tadpoles lose their tails

The tadpoles lose their tails.

Week 9 • Day 2
Sentences

---

page 111

Scarecrow Subtraction

Cross out the pictures to solve each problem.

1. 6 − 4 = 2
2. 5 − 3 = 2
3. 6 − 1 = 5
4. 4 crows are in the field.
The scarecrow scares 3 of the crows away.
How many crows are left?

4 − 3 = 1

Week 9 • Day 3
Subtraction

---

page 112

Juggling Act

Cross out. Write how many are left.

1. 3 − 1 = 2
2. 7 − 4 = 3
3. 4 − 2 = 2
4. 9 − 6 = 3
5. 5 − 3 = 2
6. 6 − 5 = 1

Week 9 • Day 3
Subtraction

---

page 113

What's New?

Each bear has something new.
To find out what it is, say the name of each picture next to the bear. Listen for the beginning sound.
Write the letter that stands for that sound under the picture.

1. h a t
2. b e l t
3. s o c k s
4. d u c k
5. d i s h

Week 9 • Day 4
Initial Consonants

---

page 114

Word Search

How many words can you find? Look for the words below and circle them.

a	n	b	e	b	i	g	f	o	r
n	a	l	o	i	s	v	u	n	m
d	p	u	g	g	o	t	n	m	a
w	q	e	b	c	n	h	l	k	k
e	r	d	c	h	e	r	j	s	e
c	f	e	i	i	h	e	i	e	u
r	u	n	t	u	p	e	s	e	t
d	o	w	n	a	m	a	k	o	n
l	w	e	r	t	o	p	m	y	t
y	o	u	m	p	l	a	y	a	m

am	at	blue	go	make	one	see	we
an	be	down	is	my	play	three	you
and	big	for	it	on	run	to	

Week 9 • Day 4
Sight Words

---

page 115

-ug Family

Put the letters together to make the -ug sound.

1. h + ug = _____
2. m + ug = _____
3. j + ug = _____ Check your child's work.
4. b + ug = _____

Look at the letters at the bottom of the page. Write them in the correct squares to finish each sentence.

5. I dug in the sand with a shovel.
6. Blankets keep us warm and snug.
7. He gave the string a tug.
8. Let's plug the hole.

| pl | d | sn | t |

Week 9 • Day 5
Word Families

---

page 116

-op Family

Put the letters together to make the -op sound.

1. t + op = _____
2. st + op = _____
3. m + op = _____ Check your child's work
4. c + op = _____

Look at the letters at the bottom of the page. Write them in the correct squares to finish each sentence.

5. He can chop wood with an axe.
6. Let's hop like rabbits.
7. The farmer had a crop of corn.
8. We shop at the mall.

| cr | sh | h | ch |

Week 9 • Day 5
Word Families

Week 10

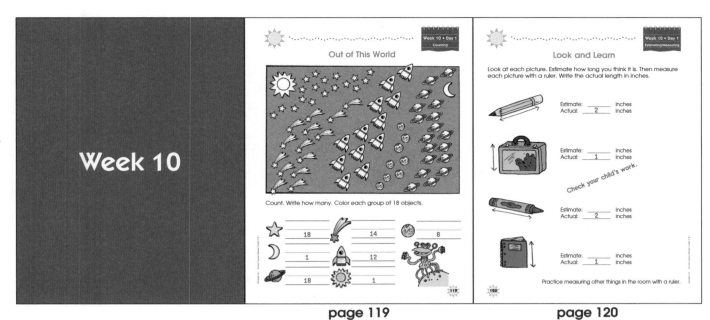

page 119

page 120

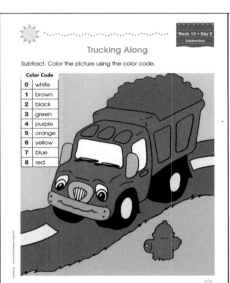

page 121

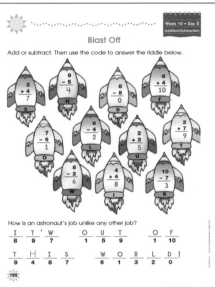

page 122

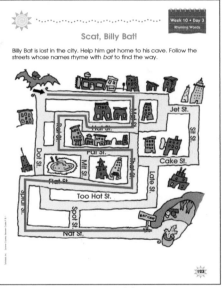

page 123

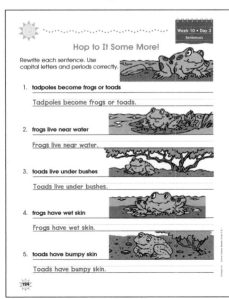

page 124

page 125

page 126

The Continents

Write the names of the continents.

Africa

Asia

Australia

Antarctica

Check your child's work.

Europe

North America

South America

Word Search

How many words can you find? Look for the words below and circle them.

t	l	r	q	p	c	d	i	d	a
h	h	i	j	k	a	y	m	n	e
e	a	t	f	g	m	z	o	f	v
r	s	h	a	v	e	d	u	o	v
e	t	e	e	d	c	c	n	u	w
u	p	y	e	s	b	a	d	r	g
v	l	b	w	o	u	t	e	d	v
w	e	x	h	o	y	z	r	i	h
r	a	q	i	n	o	w	b	n	i
o	s	p	t	c	u	k	j	t	u
n	e	m	e	l	r	s	t	o	a

came	four	into	now	please	under	white
did	have	it	on	soon	up	yes
eat	in	me	out	there	we	

---

page 127   **page 128**

THIS CERTIFIES THAT

IS NOW READY

FOR GRADE

CONGRATULATIONS!

I'm proud of you!